Prepared in cooperation with the U.S. Bureau of Reclamation

Characterization of Cyanophyte Biomass in a Bureau of Reclamation Reservoir

By Nancy S. Simon, Ahmad Abdul Ali, Kyle Michael Samperton, Charles S. Korson, Kris Fischer, and Michael L. Hughes

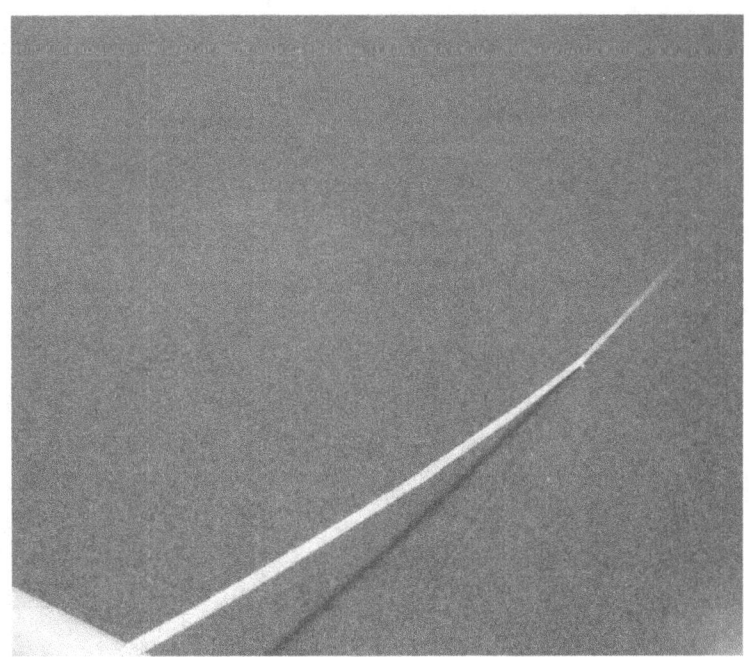

Open-File Report 2013–1156

U.S. Department of the Interior
U.S. Geological Survey

U.S. Department of the Interior
SALLY JEWELL, Secretary

U.S. Geological Survey
Suzette M. Kimball, Acting Director

U.S. Geological Survey, Reston, Virginia: 2013

For more information on the USGS—the Federal source for science about the Earth,
its natural and living resources, natural hazards, and the environment—visit
http://www.usgs.gov or call 1–888–ASK–USGS

For an overview of USGS information products, including maps, imagery, and publications,
visit *http://www.usgs.gov/pubprod*

To order this and other USGS information products, visit *http://store.usgs.gov*

Suggested citation:
Simon, N.S., Ali, A.A., Samperton, K.M., Korson, C.S., Fischer, Kris, and Hughes, M.L., 2013, Characterization of
cyanophyte biomass in a Bureau of Reclamation reservoir, U.S. Geological Survey Open-File Report 2013–1156,
59 p., http://pubs.usgs.gov/of/2013/1156.

Cover: Anchor line through *Aphanizomenon flos-aquae* in water column of Upper
Klamath Lake, Oregon, July 14, 2010. Photograph by Kyle Samperton,
U.S. Geological Survey intern (2012) for the National Association of Geoscience
Teachers.

Contents

Figures

Tables

Acknowledgments

Samples were collected from Upper Klamath Lake, Oregon, for this study by Kyle Samperton, U.S. Geological Survey intern (2012) for the National Association of Geoscience Teachers. Kyle also took the photographs of *Aphanizomenon flos-aquae* in Upper Klamath Lake, Oregon.

Boat time and sampling site identification were provided by scientists from the Klamath Tribes Research Station in Chiloquin, Oregon. s.d.g.

Conversion Factors

SI to Inch/Pound

Multiply	By	To obtain
Length		
centimeter (cm)	0.3937	inch (in.)
millimeter (mm)	0.03937	inch (in.)
meter (m)	3.281	foot (ft)
nanometer (nm)	3.3937×10^{-8}	inch (in)
Volume		
liter (L)	1.057	quart (qt)
cubic centimeters	0.033815	ounce, fluid (fl. oz)
milliliter	0.033814	ounce, fluid (fl. oz)
Mass		
gram (g)	0.03527	ounce, avoirdupois (oz)
kilogram (kg)	2.205	pound avoirdupois (lb)
milligram (mg)	3.527×10^{-5}	ounce
metric ton per year	3.527×10^{-8}	ton per year (ton/yr)
Density		
gram per cubic centimeter (g/cm^3)	62.4220	pound per cubic foot (lb/ft^3)

Temperature in degrees Celsius (°C) may be converted to degrees Fahrenheit (°F) as follows:
°F=(1.8×°C)+32
Temperature in degrees Fahrenheit (°F) may be converted to degrees Celsius (°C) as follows:
°C=(°F-32)/1.8
Vertical coordinate information is referenced to the North American Vertical Datum of 1988 (NAVD 88).
Horizontal coordinate information is referenced to the North American Datum of 1983 (NAD 83).
Altitude, as used in this report, refers to distance above the vertical datum.
*Transmissivity: The standard unit for transmissivity is cubic foot per day per square foot times foot of aquifer thickness
$[(ft^3/d)/ft^2]ft$. In this report, the mathematically reduced form, foot squared per day (ft^2/d), is used for convenience.
Specific conductance is given in microsiemens per centimeter at 25 degrees Celsius (µS/cm at 25°C).
Concentrations of chemical constituents in water are given either in milligrams per liter (mg/L) or micrograms per liter (µg/L).
NOTE TO USGS USERS: Use of hectare (ha) as an alternative name for square hectometer (hm^2) is restricted to the
measurement of small land or water areas. Use of liter (L) as a special name for cubic decimeter (dm^3) is restricted to the
measurement of liquids and gases. No prefix other than milli should be used with liter. Metric ton (t) as a name for
megagram (Mg) should be restricted to commercial usage, and no prefixes should be used with it.

Abbreviations

~	approximately
Δ	interchangeable with ppm as chemical shift unit nuclear magnetic resonance spectroscopy spectra
Δ	heat applied
μg	microgram, 1×10^{-6} gram
μL	microliter, 1×10^{-6} liter
μs	microsecond, 1×10^{-6} second
^{31}P NMR	Nuclear Magnetic Resonance spectroscopy using the isotope ^{31}P
ACS	American Chemical Society
AFA	cyanophyte, *Aphanizomenon flos-aquae*
Al	aluminum
AS	Agency Lake South, sampling location
C	carbon
^{o}C	degrees Celsius
Ca	calcium
cc	cubic centimeter
CS	chemical shift; location of peak in NMR spectrum
CWA	Clean Water Act
D_2O	deuterium oxide
DNA	deoxyribonucleic acid
EDTA	ethylenediaminetetraacetic acid; metal complexing agent
ER	Eagle Ridge, sampling location
ERS	Eagle Ridge South, sampling location
Fe	iron
g	gram
H_3PO_4	phosphoric acid
HB	Howard Bay, sampling location
Hz	hertz, the measure of the frequency of an electromagnetic wave
ICP–AES	Inductively Coupled Plasma detector for Atomic Emission Spectrometer
Inorg.	inorganic
Inter std	internal standard
IP	inorganic phosphorus
K	kilo bytes of data
M	molarity, moles per liter of solution
MDPA	methylene diphosphonic acid; internal standard for ^{31}P analysis
MDT	Mid-trench, sampling site
megohm	$10^6 \times$ SI unit for electrical resistance
mg	milligram, 10^{-3} gram
mg g^{-1}	milligrams per gram dry weight of sample
MHz	megahertz, 10^6 Hz
min	minute
mL	milliliter, 10^{-3} L
mm	millimeter, 10^{-3} m

mV	millivolts, 10^{-3} volts
nm	nanometer, 10^{-9} m
N	nitrogen
n.a.	not available
NaOH	sodium hydroxide
NBI	North Buck Island, sampling location
NMR	Nuclear Magnetic Resonance spectroscopy
^{o}C	degrees Celsius
^{o}K	degrees Kelvin; degrees Kelvin = 273 + degrees Celsius
OP	organic phosphorus
P	phosphorus
PM	Pelican Marina, sampling location
PMN	Pelican Marina North, sampling location
ppm	chemical shift unit in nuclear magnetic resonance spectroscopy spectra
RNA	ribonucleic acid
rpm	revolutions per minute
s	second
SB	Shoalwater Bay, sampling location
s.d.g.	*sola deo gloria*
soln.	solution
Ti	titanium
TP	total phosphorus
UKL	Upper Klamath Lake, Oregon
Zn	zinc
+	internal standard added
x	very small peak in spectrum

Characterization of Cyanophyte Biomass in a Bureau of Reclamation Reservoir

By Nancy S. Simon,[1] Ahmad Abdul Ali,[2] Kyle M. Samperton,[3] Charles S. Korson,[4] Kris Fischer,[5] and Michael L. Hughes[6]

Abstract

The purpose of this study was to characterize the cyanophyte *Aphanizomenon flos-aquae* (AFA) from Upper Klamath Lake, Oregon, (UKL) and, based on this description, explore uses for AFA, which would have commercial value. AFA collected from UKL in 2010 from eight sites during a period of approximately 2 weeks were similar in composition spatially and temporally. ^{31}P nuclear magnetic resonance analysis of the samples indicated that the AFA samples contained a broad range of phosphorus-containing compounds. The largest variation in organic phosphorus compounds was found in a sample collected from Howard Bay compared with samples collected the sites at Pelican Marina, North Buck Island, Eagle Ridge, Eagle Ridge South, Shoalwater Bay, and Agency Lake South. ^{31}P Nuclear Magnetic Resonance data indicated that the average ratio of inorganic phosphorus (orthophosphate) to organic phosphorus in the AFA samples was approximately 60:40 in extraction solutions of either water or a more rigorous solution of sodium hydroxide plus ethylenediaminetetraacetic acid. This indicates that when AFA cells senesce, die and lyse, cell contents added to the water column contain a broad spectrum of phosphorus-containing compounds approximately 50 percent of which are organic phosphorus compounds. The organic phosphorus content of AFA is directly and significantly related to the total carbon content of AFA. Total concentrations of the elements Al, Ca, Fe, Mg, Ti and Zn were similar in all samples with the exception of elevated iron in the July 27, 2010, sample from Pelican Marina. Iron concentration in the July 27, 2010, Pelican Marina sample was elevated; the concentration of iron in the August 9, 2010, sample from Pelican Marina was indistinguishable from iron in the other AFA samples that were collected. The carbon to nitrogen ratio in all AFA samples that were analyzed was 5.4 plus or minus 0.04 as compared with the Redfield ratio of carbon to nitrogen ratio of 6.6, which could be attributed to the large concentrations of nitrogen (protein) in AFA or to optimal growth rate.

In UKL there is a concern that microcystin, the toxin produced by microcystis, might be present in what appears to be predominantly AFA in the lake water. Experiments preformed as part of this study identified a process that reduces the toxicity of microcystin when it is present in water slurry containing

---

[1] U.S. Geological Survey, *nssimon@usgs.gov*.
[2] VirginiaTech Carilion School of Medicine
              (formerly at James Madison University).
[3] Princeton University, Princeton, New Jersey, *ksampert@princeton.edu*.
[4] U.S. Bureau of Reclamation, *ckorson@usbr.gov*.
[5] Klamath Tribe's Research Station, Chiloquin, Oregon, *fischerkris@msn.com*.
[6] Oregon Institute of Technology, Klamath Falls, Oregon, *Michael.Hughes@oit.edu*.

AFA. The process combines (1) the inhibition of the α, β-unsaturated carbonyl in microcystin with (2) the breakdown of proteins in AFA using the protease activity of plant enzymes. Protease enzymes can break peptide bonds in microcystin, which results in destruction of the cyclic structure of the microcystin polypeptide. Laboratory conditions used in this study resulted in the inactivation of approximately 60 percent of the activity of microcystin.

Introduction

High density blooms of cyanobacterial algae adversely affect water quality, fish populations, and outdoor recreation at Bureau of Reclamation reservoirs in the western United States. Algal blooms degrade water quality when algal cells senesce and deplete lentic systems of oxygen necessary for biotic organisms to survive, release toxins that can threaten aquatic life and human health, and contribute large particulate organic loads to downstream waters (Sullivan and others, 2009). It may become economically viable to remove algal biomass from Bureau of Reclamation reservoirs or downstream receiving waters in quantities sufficient to remediate ecosystem effects if commercially valuable products can be derived from cyanobacterial algae.

Bureau of Reclamation reservoirs in the western United States are often faced with water-quality impairment problems that result in Clean Water Act (CWA 303(d) listing status (California State Water Resources Control Board, 2010) for a variety of water-quality properties. Upper Klamath Lake (UKL), which is part of the Klamath Irrigation Project under the jurisdiction of the Mid-Pacific Region Klamath Basin Area Office, is a prime example of one reservoir with acute water-quality impairments and an Oregon CWA 303(d) (California State Water Resources Control Board, 2010) listing for dissolved oxygen, pH, and chlorophyll. Large populations of AFA in UKL are attributed the elevated concentrations of phosphorus (P) in the water column (Eldridge and others, 2012; Harke and others, 2012). One approach to reducing the concentrations of P and AFA in the water column is removal of AFA biomass from the lake.

Additionally, the Klamath River downstream from UKL is 303 (d) listed for nutrients, organic enrichment/dissolved oxygen, and temperature in California. More recently (2010) reaches of the Klamath River in California also have been listed for microcystin. In the case of Bureau of Reclamation's Klamath Irrigation Project, water-quality problems caused by nutrients coming from UKL are a major management concern because several fish species listed under the Federal Endangered Species Act rely on habitats in UKL (endangered Lost River and shortnose suckers) and downstream from UKL (threatened Coho salmon) in the Klamath River. Establishing commercial uses for AFA would improve the chances that a private company would be interested in removing AFA from UKL waters before they enter the Klamath River leading to an improvement of water quality in the Klamath River. This could provide direct benefits to the Klamath Irrigation Project by leading to the development of in-lake algae removal programs scaled to improve water-quality conditions in UKL.

This report presents (1) a characterization of AFA removed from the lake in the summer of 2010, and (2) a concept for breaking up protein in AFA to amino acids and reducing the toxicity of microcystin that can be found in some populations of cyanophytes growing in the water column with AFA. Any planned use of AFA for biological purposes would have to take into account the possibility that microcystin is present in the algal biomass removed from the lake.

The interest in reducing the toxicity of microcystin described in this report is focused solely on microcystin in the biomass of cyanobacteria collected from the water column. It is not focused on microcystin dissolved in the water column.

Objectives

This research is needed to explore the potential for removing cyanobacterial algae on a commercial scale with the aim of improving water-quality conditions in Bureau of Reclamation reservoirs throughout the western United States. Cyanobacterial algae removal from Bureau of Reclamation reservoirs will yield multiple benefits. Water-quality conditions, if dramatically improved, would improve habitat conditions for aquatic organisms, slow the eutrophication process, reduce nutrient loading downstream, and help the Bureau of Reclamation ensure compliance with Clean Water Act requirements and Total Maximum Daily Limits (TMDL). (California State Water Resources Control Board, 2010).

This study explores the use of cyanobacterial biomass in UKL for commercially marketable products. Removal of some fraction of this algal biomass could reduce the negative effect of algal/cyanobacterial productivity on UKL dissolved oxygen and pH and improve water-quality conditions for the federally listed Lost River and shortnose suckers in UKL and Coho salmon downstream in the Klamath River. Moreover, biomass removal would eliminate a substantial pool of nutrients in the entire Klamath River system. Large populations of AFA in UKL are attributed to the elevated concentrations of P in the water column of UKL (Eldridge and others, 2012; Harke and others, 2012). One approach to reducing the concentrations of P and AFA in the water column is removal of AFA biomass from the lake.

An objective of the study was to characterize AFA mats (dense blooms) because removal of AFA mats from the water is a more efficient method of algae removal than screening small colonies of AFA from the water column. Cyanobacteria blooms are present in other Bureau of Reclamation reservoirs and these methods are expected to have transferability to other settings.

Study Description and Methods

Study Design

To characterize AFA, this report provides the chemical composition of AFA and a description of the forms, inorganic and organic, of P in the AFA samples collected in the summer of 2010. Based on its large protein content, a promising use for AFA, was determined to be development as an agricultural feed stock. This study addressed detoxification of microcystin that might be included with AFA during AFA harvest from UKL.

Sampling Locations

AFA samples were collected from UKL, in July and August, 2010. A list of the sampling sites with collection dates and latitude/longitude values for each site appears in table 1. A map showing sampling site locations is shown in figure 1. The sampling locations for this study were selected from a list of established sampling sites where water quality samples are routinely collected by Klamath Tribes Research Station field personnel (Walker and others, 2012).

Sample Collection

AFA sample collection was opportunistic. AFA material was collected when and where a surface bloom was present. A plastic sieve with a 0.5 millimeter (mm mesh screen was used to lift the floating algal mat from the water to the shipboard (fig. 2). The material in the sieve was transferred to a gallon-size plastic zip-lock bag. The plastic bags containing AFA samples were placed in a cooler with ice and shipped the day of collection using overnight shipping service to the laboratory in Reston, Virginia, where they were frozen.

A separate sample of AFA was collected on August 30, 2011, to be used for laboratory studies. This sample of AFA was collected at the water surface near the mid-trench site located near Eagle Ridge (fig. 1). The algae was freeze-dried and stored at -10 degrees Celsius (^{o}C).

Sample Preparation

Frozen AFA was thawed and refrozen 3 times. This was done to maximize the lysing of the AFA cells, which breaks cell walls to expose cell contents for chemical analysis. After the third freeze-thaw cycle the AFA was transferred to glass jar(s) and refrozen. The frozen AFA was lyophilized. The dry AFA in screw cap glass jars was stored at -10 ^{o}C.

Sample Analysis

^{31}P Nuclear Magnetic Resonance (NMR) Analysis

Aliquots of the AFA were extracted with three different extraction solutions for ^{31}P NMR analysis. One-tenth gram (g) of freeze-dried AFA was extracted with the following solutions:

1. 20 milliliters (mL) of 0.25 molar (M) NaOH plus 0.05 M EDTA. An internal standard is added before lyophilization Internal standards in NMR are used to quantify peaks in spectra of unknowns. An internal standard and the P-containing compounds in the sample will respond similarly to variations in the working conditions of the instrument. The concentration of the standard is known and this concentration is divided by the area of the peak produced by the internal standard to give a concentration per unit peak area. This value is used to quantify the peaks of the unknown. The peak of the internal standard should not have the same chemical shift as any peaks that appear in the spectrum of the unknown.

2. 20 mL of 18 megohm water, and

3. 20 mL of 18 megohm water (Internal standard added before lyophilization).

Extraction with 0.25 M NaOH plus 0.05 M EDTA is the typical extraction solution for the preparation of ^{31}P NMR samples because this solution extracts a maximum of P-containing compounds in biological samples (Cade-Menun and Preston, 1996).

A comparison with water was chosen to demonstrate the compounds of P that are released to the water column when AFA cells die and lyse adding cell contents to surrounding water. Because phosphonate compounds of P have been found in cyanobacteria samples, extractions were prepared without and with the internal standard, which is a phosphonate compound. Absence of internal standard avoided overlap of the peak from the internal standard with a peak from phosphonate in the sample. The spectrum of the sample to which internal standard was added could be quantified by using the ratio of known concentration of the internal standard to its peak area.

At the end of a 16 hour extraction period, the samples were centrifuged at 2,500 revolutions per minute (rpm) for 20 minutes (min). The supernatant was pipetted to a glass jar. An internal standard of methylene diphosphonic acid (50 micrograms (µg) P) was added to the supernatant from extraction steps (1) and (3). The contents of the jar were frozen, and lyophilized.

The dried extracts from treated samples were transferred to 2-cubic centimeters (cc) centrifuge tubes in the Reston laboratory. At the James Madison University Shenandoah Regional NMR Facility located at James Madison University, the material in the centrifuge tube was dissolved with a combination of 0.675 mL of 0.25 M NaOH–0.05 M EDTA and 0.2-mL of 10 M NaOH in D$_2$O (99.9

percent deuterium oxide, Sigma-Aldrich) immediately before analysis. The solution was mixed for ~2 min by using a vortex shaker, centrifuged and pipetted into 5 mm NMR tubes. The ^{31}P NMR measurements were carried out on a Bruker Avance, 600 MHz (megahertz) spectrometer, equipped with a 5-mm broad band tunable probe operating at 242.9 MHz frequency for [31]P. The proton decoupled spectra were acquired with a 30° pulse width (3.25 microseconds (μs)), acquisition time 1.35 second (s), relaxation delay 1 s, and sweep width 24,350 Hz (100 ppm). The sample temperature was maintained at 293 °K (Kelvin) throughout the acquisition of 8,000 to 25,600 pulses, as required to achieve acceptable signal to noise ratio. The 64-K (64 kilobytes) data point file was processed with 3 Hz line broadening and transformed to produce a 32-K data point spectrum. The chemical shifts were indirectly referenced to external 85% phosphoric acid (H_3PO_4) (at δ=0.; at chemical shift=0) by way of the lock signal. Spectral processing was performed with Bruker-BioSpin's TopSpin 1.3 software.

Peak assignments in the ^{31}P spectra that were obtained were made by using chemical shift data reported by Koopmans and others (2003); Turner et al. (2003); Cade-Menun (2005); and from ^{31}P NMR experiments in the James Madison University laboratory. Chemical shift data are sensitive to solution pH. The relative separation of chemical shifts for P-containing compounds is more reproducible than the absolute values for chemical shifts for P-containing compounds. To compare NMR data from multiple studies, orthophosphate values are normalized to a chosen value and the chemical shifts for compounds flanking orthophosphate are calculated based on the arithmetic difference between the chemical shift value obtained for orthophosphate in the reported study and the chemical shift reported for orthophosphate in studies described in the literature.

Carbon and Nitrogen Analysis

Algal samples were analyzed for total carbon (C) and total nitrogen (N) by using 20 milligrams (mg) freeze-dried AFA. Flash oxidation of each sample was followed by separation of the gaseous products using a Carlo Erba EA 1108 Elemental Analyzer.

Total Elemental Analysis

Samples weighing 0.07 to 0.1 g were digested in concentrated nitric and hydrofluoric acids by using microwave digestion equipment (Simon and others, 2009). Hydrofluoric acid was used in addition to nitric acid because it is possible that diatoms were included in the whole mat sample. An acid blank and reference standard Community Bureau of Reference BCR® - 60 certified Reference Material (aquatic plant, *Lagarosiphon major*) (European Commission, 2007) were included with each set of sediment digests. Ten milliliters (mL) of concentrated nitric acid were added approximately 16 hours before 2 mL of hydrofluoric acid were added to the Teflon vessels containing the weighed AFA samples. Soaking the samples in nitric acid helped wet the samples. The penetration of sample particles with acid contributes to efficient dissolution of sample particles. Immediately after addition of hydrofluoric acid, the vessels were closed, placed in the instrument round table, and placed in a CEM Microwave Accelerated Reaction System (MARS). After the digestion sequence in the microwave, the samples were brought up to a volume of 100 mL using double deionized water.

Diluted aliquots of microwave digests of AFA samples were analyzed for P concentrations by using the method of Murphy and Riley (1962). Microwave digests were diluted 1:20 with 0.5 percent nitric acid and analyzed for Al, Ca, Fe, Mg, Ti, and Zn by using a Perkin-Elmer Model 5100 Inductively Coupled Plasma-Atomic Emission spectrometer ICP–AES.

Data from a set of microwave digestion samples were considered acceptable if the data for a sample of the aquatic plant, *Lagarosiphon major* BCR® 60, certified Reference Material (European

Commission, 2007) analyzed with the set of sediment samples were within two standard deviations of the certified values reported for the standard.

Conversion of AFA Protein to Amino acids and Inactivation of Microcystin

Aliquots from one large sample of freeze-dried AFA were used for all experiments. The AFA was collected from Upper Klamath Lake, Oregon, on August 30, 2011, and shipped to the laboratory in Reston, Va. The bulk AFA was frozen and lyophilized upon arrival at the laboratory. This material was stored in a glass jar at -10 $^{\circ}$C. All experiments combined 0.1 g of freeze dried AFA with 20 mL of water. When testing the effect of experimental conditions on concentrations of microcystin, 1 microgram (µg) of microcystin in 1 mL methanol was added to AFA slurries.

Bromelain is a protease enzyme that will break down large protein molecules to short chain polypeptides and amino acids. Microcystin is a polypeptide and AFA contains approximately 60 percent protein. This study examined the efficiency of bromelain in degrading the proteins in AFA and breaking down the microcystin molecule. Cysteine was added to increase the activity of bromelain. In these experiments 0.1 g of bromelain and 0.1 g of cysteine were added to slurries of AFA when studying the effects of enzyme digestion on the concentration of microcystin in the mixture. Digestions were run in a rotating flask in a water bath at 60°C for a period of 1 hour. At the end of the digestions, the sample in the flask was transferred to test tubes and centrifuged for 20 minutes at 2,500 rpm. The supernatant was freeze dried and extracted with 5 mL of methanol.

Analysis for Microcystin in Extracts of AFA

The method used for the detection of microcystin is based on the method published by Lo and others (2002). This method is an electrochemical technique that can be used for detecting and quantifying analytes in complex environmental samples because the detector that applies 300 millivolts (mV) in this analysis is 'blind' to most compounds in environmental samples which require larger potentials for oxidation.

This method uses the reaction between α, β−unsaturated carbonyl functional groups and 6-ferrocentylhexanthiol. All homologs of microcystin contain a α, β−unsaturated carbonyl functional group so this method is sensitive to all homologs of microcystin present in a sample. The published method (Lo and others, 2002) was developed for use with solutions of microcystin. In this study the method was expanded for use with methanol extracts of protease digests of AFA.

Chemicals used in the study experiments were American Chemical Society (ACS) grade with the following exceptions, bromelain, microcystin-LR and 6-ferrocentylhexanthiol (Sigma Chemicals). High purity methanol was required. Other sources of methanol contained electroactive species that produced a high background in the solvent and interfering peaks in the chromatograms when samples dissolved in methanol were injected.

Instrumentation: A Bioanalytical Systems liquid chromatograph with an electrochemical detector was operated at 300 mV. Initially, chromatographs were obtained by using a trichloroacetic acid eluent at a pH of 2. Because the electrochemical reaction in this method is oxidation, the buffer was changed to ammonium acetate at a pH of 5. Concentrations of buffer ranging from 0.05 to 0.2 were tested and ratios of methanol concentrations of 35 to 50 percent were compared. The most effective buffer for separating the components of the samples was a 1:1 ratio of 0.05 M ammonium acetate buffer at a pH of 5.0 and methanol.

Several chromatographic columns were tested. A low-flow rate is required for a good separation of the peaks produced when AFA extract samples are injected onto the column. An Agilent Zorbax Poroshell 120 SB-C18 column (2.1x30 mm, 2.7-micron particles) gave the best separation of microcystin in AFA extracts within a one-half hour time period when the eluent flow is 0.2 cc per min and the column was heated to 70 °C.

    Instrument working conditions
    Electrode: 300 mV
    Eluent: 50% 0.05 M ammonium acetate pH 5.0: 50% methanol
    Flow: 0.2 mL per minute
    Column heater: 70° C
    Injection loop: 20 microliters (µL)

Coomassie Analysis for Protein Concentration in Digests of AFA

The method published by Bradford (1976) was used to determine the percent change of proteins in AFA to polypeptides and amino acids during protease digestion. The Coomassie Brilliant Blue dye has the formula $C_{47}H_{48}N_3NaO_7S_2$ and formula weight 854.02. When mixed with a protein solution, an acidic Coomassie-dye reagent changes color from brown to blue in proportion to the amount of protein present in the sample. Protein determinations are made by comparison of the color response of the sample at wavelengths 610 (nanometer) nm and 595 nm. The smaller the difference of the absorbance of the sample at the two wavelengths, the smaller the concentration of protein in the sample. The Coomassie blue dye reagent is made by diluting 10 mg Coomassie Brilliant Blue dye in 5 mL of ethanol plus 10 mL of phosphoric acid to 100 mL with water. To 5 mL of this solution, 100 µL of AFA digest was added. The AFA digests were 0.1 g samples of AFA in 20 mL of water that were (a) not heated, (b) heated to 60° C for 1 hour, or (c) heated to 60 °C for 1 hour with 0.1g cysteine and 0.1g bromelain

Results and Discussion

31P NMR Analysis

Nuclear magnetic resonance (NMR) is a form of absorption spectrometry similar to infrared or ultraviolet spectrometry (Silverstein and others, 1974). Like other methods of spectrometry, NMR measures the interaction between molecules with energies from the electromagnetic spectrum. Under appropriate conditions in NMR, a sample can absorb electromagnetic radiation in the radio-frequency region at frequencies governed by the characteristics of the sample. Chemical shift is the difference in the frequency of absorption of a reference proton and the frequency of absorption of a proton in the compound being analyzed. The applied frequency used in the analysis must be given as hertz, if the chemical shift is not calculated by dividing the frequency at which the peak from the compound appeared, by the applied frequency, and multiplying by 10^6. The units of chemical shift from this calculation are δ (dimensionless) or parts per million (ppm). Energy absorption is a function of certain nuclei in the molecule. A plot of the frequencies of the absorption peaks as compared to peak intensities constitutes an NMR spectrum. (Silverstein and others, 1974). Chemical shift data for multiple ^{31}P-containing functional groups are listed in table 2. An ideal spectrum of P-containing compounds is shown in figure 3.

The ^{31}P data in table 3 are from the samples collected for this study. The table includes chemical shift (CS, position of peaks in the NMR spectrum) data based on normalization of other peaks with the peak for orthophosphate in each spectrum, and peak area and concentration calculations based on an internal standard. The ratios of concentrations of inorganic and organic P in all NMR spectra averaged 3:2. Slightly smaller concentrations of organic P were extracted by water than were extracted by 0.25 M NaOH plus 0.05 M EDTA.

All of the spectra for the AFA samples collected for this study are presented in figure 4. A comparison of these spectra with the descriptive ^{31}P NMR spectrum presented in figure. 3 (Cade-Menun, 2005) indicates that a suite of organic P compounds are present in AFA cells. The one organic P compound that was observed in only two (Howard Bay and Eagle Ridge) of the nine AFA samples was polyphosphate. Biological organisms use polyphosphates to store surplus phosphate. No phosphonate was observed in samples that did not contain the internal standard used in our studies. The largest inorganic peaks were orthophosphate monoesters, which include phosphate sugars (glucose-phosphate), phospholipids, and phytic acid. Orthophosphate diesters include deoxyribonucleic acid (DNA) and ribonucleic acid (RNA).

Included in figure 4 are three ^{31}P NMR spectra for each AFA sample. The first extraction was done by using 0.25 M NaOH plus 0.05 M EDTA, which extracts a maximum of the P-containing compounds in biological samples. This is the typical extraction solution for the preparation of ^{31}P samples. The samples contain the internal standard methylene diphosphonic acid (MDPA) and the chemical shifts (peak position) for peaks in these spectra are directly comparable with spectra from other laboratories. ^{31}P NMR data for algae in the literature are dominated by studies of marine organisms. A limited amount of data exists for freshwater algae. The few studies of freshwater cyanophytes that have been published focus on a limited number of P-containing compounds. Selig and others (2002), for example, used ^{31}P NMR to study polyphosphates and phospholipids in the cyanophyte algae in Lake Bützow (Germany). Selig and others interpreted the presence of polyphosphate in the algae as an indicator that there was adequate phosphate for algal growth. In Upper Klamath Lake, polyphosphates were found only in samples from the Howard Bay and Eagle Ridge sampling sites.

The second and third extractions were done by using deionized water. The same internal standard (MDPA) that was added to the 0.25 M NaOH plus 0.05 M EDTA extraction was added to one of the two water extractions; no internal standard was added to the second water extraction. Using water as an extractant indicated which P-containing compounds would be released to the water column when the AFA senesced and cells lysed. In general, the pattern in spectra from 0.25 M NaOH plus 0.05 M EDTA extractions matched the spectra from the water extractions for each sample. The single exception was for the P compound, pyrophosphate, which did not appear in spectra of water extracts. Pyrophosphates are generally considered stable in water solution. Polyphosphates are not stable in 0.25 M NaOH plus 0.05 M EDTA extraction solutions of environmental samples (Hupfer, 1995) and the pyrophosphate in the 0.25 M NaOH plus 0.05 M EDTA extractions might have formed by the degradation of polyphosphates in the AFA samples.

^{31}P NMR analyses of the samples indicated that the largest variation in organic P compounds were determined in a sample collected from Howard Bay compared with samples collected the sites at Pelican Marina, Buck Island, Shoalwater Bay, and Agency Lake South. All P-containing compounds that appear in the ideal ^{31}P NMR spectrum (fig. 3) also appear in spectrum 13, Howard Bay (fig. 5). The phosphonate shown in spectrum 13 is the internal standard. The AFA in UKL is a rich source of inorganic and organic P-containing compounds.

When the AFA population senesces and the cells lyse, inorganic and organic P are released to the water column. The form of P preferentially used as a nutrient by AFA is inorganic P, that is, orthophosphate. Microcystis is able to use inorganic and organic P. The enrichment of the water column with inorganic P and organic P could favor the development of populations of microcystis (Vahtera and others, 2007; Shi and others, 2011; Eldridge and others, 2012). This might help to explain the pattern of algal species development in UKL. After the senescence of the first large AFA bloom of the summer, numbers of microcystis cells increase resulting in microcystis developing into a substantial percentage of water column phytoplankton (Eldridge and others, 2012). Possibly the enrichment of the water column with inorganic and organic P when an AFA bloom dies and the availability of organic P for microcystis growth are reasons for the increased numbers of microcystis cells in the water column of UKL.

Carbon and Nitrogen Analyses

Chemical data for AFA collected in July–August 2010 from Upper Klamath Lake, Oregon, are presented in table 4. The average concentration of carbon in the AFA samples analyzed in this study was 44 percent. The average concentration of nitrogen in the AFA samples analyzed in this study was 9.5 percent. Multiplying by the factor 6.25 (protein is 16 percent nitrogen), gives an average concentration of protein in our AFA samples of 59 percent. The organic P content of AFA is directly and significantly related to the total carbon content of AFA (fig. 6).

The carbon to nitrogen ratio in all AFA samples that were analyzed was 5.4 plus or minus 0.04 compared with the Redfield ratio of carbon to nitrogen, which is 6.6. This difference could be related to the large concentration of protein in AFA or to an optimal growth rate of AFA. Benthic algae (including cyanophytes) have been reported to produce C:N ratios that decreased with increasing growth rate (Hillebrand and Sommer, 1999).

Total Elemental Analysis

Chemical data for AFA collected in July–August 2010 from Upper Klamath Lake, Oregon, are presented in table 4. Total concentrations of P, Al, Ca, Fe, Mg, P, Ti and Zn were similar in all AFA samples analyzed in this study. The one exception was the Fe concentrations in the Pelican Marina samples collected on July 27, 2010. Iron concentrations were approximately 6 to10 times larger than in any other AFA samples including the sample from Pelican Marina collected on August 9, 2010. Titanium analyses were included in the suite of metals to identify samples that might have suspended sediment included in the algal mat. Inclusion of suspended sediment is not indicated for any of the samples.

Conversion of AFA Protein to Amino Acids and Inactivation of Microcystin

Two potential uses for AFA were considered and dismissed because results were not promising. The oil content of AFA is small, approximately 3 percent. This portends a low return for development of a biofuel. Attempts to ferment AFA in the laboratory were unsuccessful. The use of AFA for ethanol production was set aside. The use of AFA as a food stock was more promising and experiments to determine the usefulness of AFA as a protein or amino acid source were run.

Cyanophytes contain L-amino acids and D-amino acids, which sets them apart from most biological organisms, which contain only L-amino acids (Lam and others, 2009). We did not investigate the possibility that AFA might be a commercial source of D-amino acids.

AFA cells contain more than 50 percent protein. Using study data (table 4) for the average percent nitrogen in samples, the average protein content in AFA samples is calculated to be 59 percent. Based on the large concentration of protein in AFA, we decided to examine the use of AFA for animal feed.

Because microcystis, a source of the toxin microcystin, is often found growing with AFA in UKL, there is a persistent concern that microcystin could be present in AFA harvested from the lake. Our approach to determining a method to remove microcystis from AFA biomass was to consider only procedures that would make the AFA end-product suitable for use as a feed stock. The toxicity of microcystin is attributed to several structural features of the microcystin molecule (fig. 7) as listed below:

1. Microcystin inactivates phosphatase enzymes. It does this when the α, β–unsaturated carbonyl functional group of microcystin binds with sulfur-containing amino acids in phosphatase molecules (Billam, 2006).

2. The Adda group, 3-amino-9-methoxy-2,6,8-trimethyl-10-phenyl-4,6-decadienoic acid, in the microcystin molecule is considered toxic.

3. The cyclic structure of the microcystin molecule is reported to contribute to the toxicity of the molecule.

Several treatments of microcystin in slurry of AFA were tested in an effort to minimize the toxicity of the microcystin molecule. These treatments include the following:

1. Complexation of the active functional group, α, β–unsaturated carbonyl, by a compound containing a sulfydryl group was done to inactivate the α, β–unsaturated carbonyl in microcystin. Cysteine has been reported to detoxify microcystin (Zhang-Qiang, 2012).

2. The toxicity of the Adda group is linked with the loss of toxicity of the microcystin molecule when that Adda functional group is destroyed by using very strong oxidizing agents such as chlorine gas or ozone. When the Adda group is destroyed by using these strong oxidizers, the α, β–unsaturated carbonyl functional group also will be destroyed. Publications have not reported using a procedure where the Adda group was destroyed while leaving the α, β–unsaturated carbonyl functional group unaffected. Also, one study indicated that toxicity was not connected with the Adda group (Harada and others, 2004).

3. The methods that have success in degrading microcystin have generally been complex or expensive or both. Microcystin is a peptide. In the literature, reports of proteases being been used to decompose microcystin, animal proteases were used because the question being addressed was whether microcystin could be broken down in the digestive tract of an animal (Rohrlack and others, 2004). In published reports (Bourne and others, 1996) the animal proteases used in the studies have had limited effectiveness in breaking down the microcystin molecule. In this study, plant proteases were tested. Plant proteases (including bromelain and papain, which were activated with cysteine) were tested and both were determined to be effective in breaking down proteins in AFA. Bromelain was selected for detailed work because it is particularly effective in breaking arginine peptide bonds (Chloe and others, 2006). Arginine is one of the L-amino acids in the cyclic ring structure of microcystin.

In this study, the activity of microcystin is considered to be related to active α, β–unsaturated carbonyl functional groups in the microcystin molecule. Deactivation of the α, β–unsaturated carbonyl destroys the toxicity of the microcystin molecule. Using experimental conditions in this study (bromelain plus cysteine), the average loss of active microcystin at a concentration of 1 μg of microcystin in a water slurry of AFA was approximately 60 percent (table 5). Preliminary experimental results indicate that cysteine plays a role in the inactivation of microcystin. Whereas the average inactivation of microcystin in solution is approximately 60 percent using bromelain or cysteine (table 5), cysteine alone inactivated approximately 30 percent of 1 μg of microcystin in an AFA slurry (data not shown).

A common analytical procedure for the analysis of microcystin is liquid-chromatography mass-spectroscopy. Liquid-chromatography mass-spectroscopy instrumentation was not available in the Reston, Va. Biogeochemistry Lab. This complication, coupled with the need for instrumentation that could be used immediately after a digestion was completed, dictated that a sensitive analytical technique be available in our laboratory. The electrochemical technique was chosen because the derivatization step provides an electroactive form of the analyte detectable at small concentrations and employs a low voltage to the electrochemical cell making the detector 'blind' to compounds in complex extraction solutions that could complicate a chromatogram.

Coomassie Analysis for Protein Concentration in Digests of AFA

Using the Coomassie protein analysis, protein determinations were made for water slurries of AFA, and for water slurries that had been heated, and with water slurries that were heated with bromelain and cysteine. Compared with the AFA sample that was not heated; the AFA sample that was heated lost 15 percent of the protein in the sample, and the AFA sample that was heated with cysteine and bromelain lost 99 percent of the protein in the sample.

Summary

The *Aphanizomenon flos-aquae* (AFA) bloom in 2010 started to develop in the middle of July. The chemical data from all AFA samples collected from Upper Klamath Lake, Oregon, in 2010 were similar in composition spatially and temporally. The lack in temporal variability might reflect the fact that all of the samples collected for this study were collected between the end of July and the middle of August.

The carbon to nitrogen ratio in all AFA samples that were analyzed was 5.4 ± 0.04 as compared with the Redfield ratio of 6.6 for carbon to nitrogen ratio, which could be related to the large concentrations of proteins in AFA or to optimal growth rate for AFA.

^{31}P Nuclear Magnetic Resonance data indicated that both inorganic and organic phosphorus were present in AFA samples that were collected in August and September 2010, at an approximate average ratio of 3:2. This was true for all nine samples collected at different sites on dates in August and September 2010. The ratio of inorganic to organic phosphorus in AFA might be related to the pattern of algae growth in Upper Klamath Lake when a substantial growth of microcystis follows the senescence of a large population of AFA. AFA favors inorganic phosphorus as a nutrient, whereas microcystin can readily breakdown organic phosphorus as well as use inorganic phosphorus. The phosphorus contents of lysed AFA cells might favor the growth of microcystis.

The experimental conditions used in this study indicated that the average deactivation of 1 microgram of microcystin in water slurries of AFA was approximately 60 percent. The experimental conditions include a combination of the protease bromelain and the amino acid cysteine.

Laboratory studies to examine the possibility of using a plant protease and sulfhydryl-containing compound to (a) detoxify microcystin that might be present in AFA collected from the water column, and (b) break down proteins in AFA to short chain peptides and amino acids, indicate that both goals are achievable.

References Cited

Billam, M., 2006, Development and validation of microcystin biomarkers for exposure studies: Texas Tech University, Lubbock, Texas, PhD. dissertation in Department of Environmental Toxicology , 234 p. (Also available at *repositories.tdl.org/ttu-ir/handle/2346/1071.*)

Bourne, D.G., Jones, G.J., Blakeley, R.L., Jones, A., Negrl, A. P. and Riddle, P. 1996, Enzymatic Pathway for the bacterial degradation of the cyanobacterial cyclic peptide toxin microcystin LR: Applied and Environmental Microbiology v. 62 p. 4086–4094 (Also available at *http://aem.asm.org/content/62/11/4086.full.pdf.*)

Bradford, M.M., 1976, A rapid and sensitive method for the quantitation of microgram quantities of protein utilizing the principle of protein-dye binding: Analytical Biochemistry, v. 72, p. 248–254. (Also available at *http://dx.doi.org/10.1016/0003-2697(76)90527-3.*)

Cade-Menun, B.J., 2005, Characterizing phosphorus in environmental and agricultural samples by ^{31}P nuclear magnetic resonance spectroscopy: Talanta, v. 66, p. 359–371 (Also available at *http://dx.doi.org/10.1016/j.talanta.2004.12.024.*)

Cade-Menun, B. J., and Preston, C. M., 1996, A comparison of soil extraction procedures for ^{31}P NMR spectroscopy: Soil Science, v. 161 p. 770–785.

California State Water Resources Control Board, 2010, Final Klamath River TMDL action plan and basin plan amendment language for the Klamath River site specific objectives for dissolved oxygen, accessed May 8, 2013, at *http://www.waterboards.ca.gov/northcoast/water_issues/programs/tmdls/klamath_river/.*

Chloe, Y., Lleonetti, F., Greenbaum, D. C., Lecaille, F., Bogyo, M., Brömme, D., Ellman, J.A., and Craik, C.S., 2006, Substrate profiling of cysteine proteases using a combinatorial peptide library identifies functionally unique specificities: The Journal of Biological Chemistry, v. 281, p. 12,824–12,832. (Also available at *http://dx.doi.org/10.1074/jbc.M513331200* and *http://www.renyi.hu/~stipsicz/Mezo_DECEMBER/Rozsa_cikkek/9A29D09Bd01.pdf.*)

Eldridge, S.L.C., Wood, T.M., and Echols, K.R., 2012, Spatial and temporal dynamics of cyanotoxins and their relation to other water-quality variables in Upper Klamath Lake, Oregon., 2007–09: U.S. Geological Survey Scientific Investigations Report 2012–5069, 34 p. (Also available at *http://pubs.usgs.gov/sir/2012/5069/pdf/sir20125069.pdf*)

European Commission, Institute for Reference Materials and Measurements, Unit for reference materials, 2007, Certified Reference Material BCR® - 60, Certified Reference Material, Certificate of Analysis: 2440 Geel, Belgium , European Commission, Joint Research Centre, Institute for Reference Materials and Measurements (IRMM), Retieseweg 111. (Also available at *http://www.lgcstandards.com/WebRoot/Store/Shops/LGC/FilePathPartDocuments/ST-WB-CERT-1074547-1-1-1.PDF.*)

Fewer, D.P., Rouhiainen, L., Jokela, J., Wahlsten, M., Laakso, K., Wang, H. and Sivonen, K., 2007, BMC Evolutionary Biology, v. 7, p.183-193, doi:10.1186/1471-2148-7-183.

Harada, K., Imanishi, S., Kato, H., Mizuno, M., Ito, E., *and* Tsuji, K., 2004, Isolation of Adda from microcystin-LR by microbial degradation: Toxicon, v. 44, p. 107–109. (Also available at *http://dx.doi.org/10.1016/j.toxicon.2004.04.003.*)

Harke, M.J., Berry, D.L., Ammerman, J.W., and Gobler, C. J., 2012, Molecular response of the bloom-forming cyanobacterium, microcystis aeruginosa, to phosphorus limitation: Microbial Ecology, v. 63, p. 188–198. (Also available at *http://dx.doi.org/10.1007/s00248-011-9894-8* and *http://link.springer.com/article/10.1007%2Fs00248-011-9894-8#.*)

Hillebrand, H., and Sommer, U., 1999, The nutrient stoichiometry of benthic microalgal growth—Redfield proportions are optimal: Limnology and Oceanography, v. 44, no. 2, p. 440–446.

Hupfer, M., Gachter, R., and Ruegger, H., 1995, Polyphosphate in Lake Sediment—^{31}P NMR spectroscopy as a tool for its identification: Limnology and Oceanography, v. 40, p. 610–617. (Also available at *http://www.jstor.org/stable/2838175.*)

Koopmans, G.F., Chardon, W.J., Dolfing, J., Oenema, O., van der Meer, P., and van Riemsdijk, W. H., 2003, Wet chemical and phosphorus-31 nuclear magnetic resonance analysis of phosphorus speciation in sandy soil receiving long-term fertilizer or animal manure applications: Journal of Environmental Quality, v. 32, p. 287–295 (Also available at *http://dx.doi.org/10.2134/jeq2003.2870 and https://www.agronomy.org/publications/jeq/abstracts/32/1/287.*)

Lam, H., Oh, D-C., Cava, F., Takacs, C.N. , Clardy, J., de Pedro, M. A., and Waldor, M.K., 2009, D-amino acids govern stationary phase cell wall remodeling in bacteria, Science, v. 325, p. 1,552–1,555 (Available at *http://www.sciencemag.org/content/325/5947/1552.full.pdf.*)

Lo, K. K-W., Ng, D. C-M., Lau, J. S-Y., Wu, R. S-S., and Lam P. K-S., 2002, Derivatization of microcystin with a redox-active label for high performance liquid chromatography/electrochemical detection: New Journal of Chemistry, v. 27, p. 274–279. (Available at *http://dx.doi.org/10.1039/b206384k.*)

Murphy, J., and Riley, J.P., 1962, A modified single solution method for the determination of phosphate in natural waters: Analytical Chemical Acta, v. 27, p. 31–36. (Also available at http://www.sciencedirect.com/science/article/pii/S0003267000884445.

Rohrlack, T., Christoffersen, K., Kaebernick, M., and Neilan, 2004, Cyanobacterial protease inhibitor microviriden J causes a lethal molting disruption in *Daphnia pulicaria*: Applied and Environmental Microbiology, v. 70, p. 5047-5050.

Selig, U., Hübener, T., and Michalik, M., 2002, Dissolved and particulate phosphorus forms in a eutrophic shallow lake: Aquatic Science, v.64, p. 97–105. (Also available at *http://www.lu.lv/ecotox/publikacijas-3-kursa-studentiem/Phosphorous.pdf.*)

Shi, X, Qian, S., Kong, F., Zhang, M., and Yu, Y., 2011, Differences in growth and alkaline phosphatase activity between *Microcystis aeruginosa* and *Chlorella pyrenoidosa* in response to media with different organic phosphorus: Journal of Limnology, v.70, p. 21–25. (Also available at *http://dx.doi.org/10.3274/JL11-70-1-04.*)

Silverstein, R.M., Bassler, G.C., and Morrill, R., 1974, Spectrometric identification of organic compounds, (3d): New York. John Wiley and Sons, p.159–164.

Simon, N.S., Lynch, D., and Gallaher, T.N., 2009, Phosphorus fractionation in sediment cores collected in 2005 before and after onset of an *Aphanizomenon flos-aquae* bloom in Upper Klamath Lake, OR, USA: Water Air Soil Pollution, v. 204, p. 139–153 (Also available at *http://dx.doi.org/10.1007/s11270-009-0033-9 and http://link.springer.com/article/10.1007/s11270-009-0033-9?null#page-1.*)

Sullivan, A.B., Snyder, D.M., and Rounds, S.A., 2009, Controls on biochemical oxygen demand in the upper Klamath River, Oregon Chemical Geology, v. 269, p. 12-21.
Available at *http://or.water.usgs.gov/proj/keno_reach/download/chemgeo_bod_final.pdf*

Turner, B.L, Mahieu, N., and Condron, L.M., 2003, Phosphorus-31 nuclear magnetic resonance spectral assignments of phosphorus compounds in soil NaOH/EDTA extracts: Soil Science Society of America Journal, v. 67, p. 497–510. (Also available at *http://hdl.handle.net/10182/1304 and http://researcharchive.lincoln.ac.nz/dspace/handle/10182/1304.*)

Vahtera, E., Laamanen, M., and Rintala, J.-M., 2007, Use of different phosphorus sources by the bloom-forming cyanobacteria *Aphanizomenon flos-aquae* and *Nodularia spumigena*: Aquatic Microbial Ecology, v. 46, p. 225–237. (Also available *http://www.int-res.com/articles/ame2006/46/a046p225.pdf.*)

Walker, W.W., Walker, J.D., and Kann, J., 2012, Evaluation of water and nutrient balances for the Upper Klamath Lake Basin in water years 1992–2010: Aquatic Ecosystems Sciences, LLC and W. Walker, PhD., and J. Walker, M., Engineer, Environmental Engineers, 50 p.

Zhang-Qiang, D., Xie, P., Deng, X., Chen, J., and Dai, M., 2012, The role of cysteine conjugation in the detoxification of microcystin-LR in liver of bighead carp (*Aristichthys nobilis*)—A field and laboratory study: Ecotoxicology, v.21, p. 244–252. (Also available at *http://dx.doi.org/10.1007/s10646-011-0783-1.*)

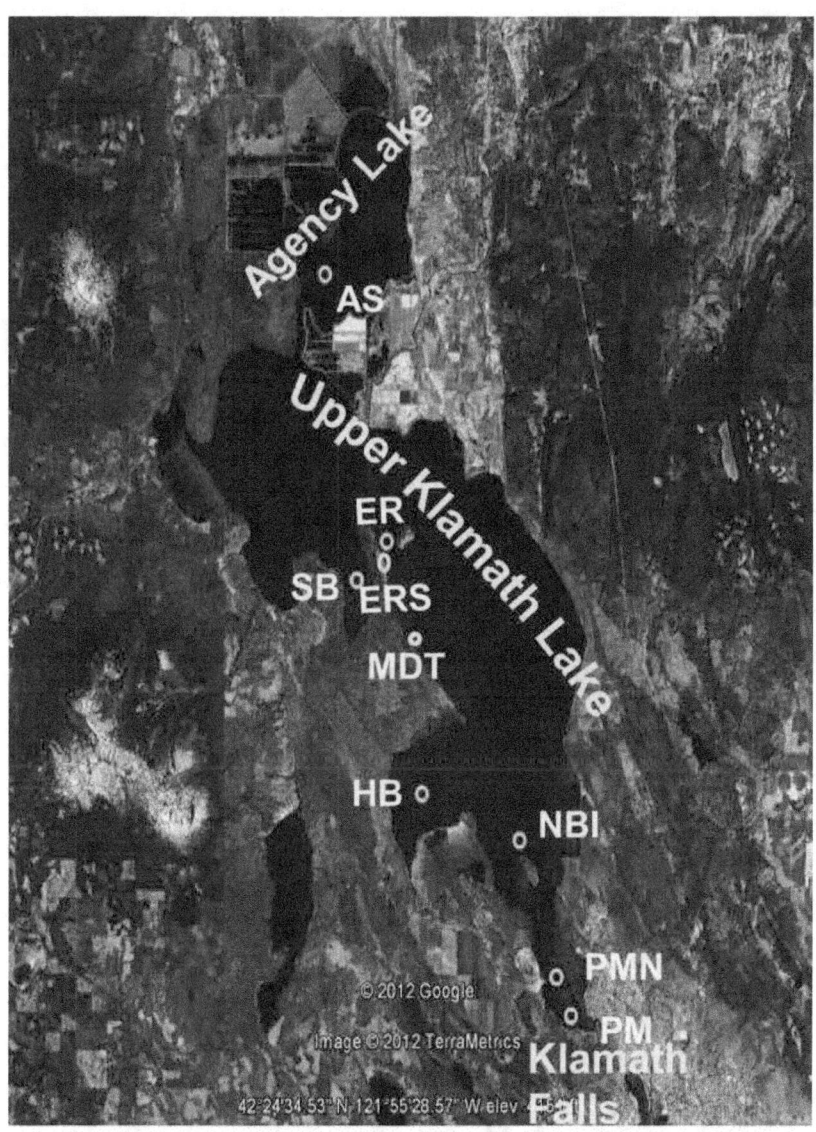

Figure 1. Map of Upper Klamath Lake, Oregon, showing sampling sites for *Aphanizomenon flos-aquae* (AFA) collected in July and August, 2010. Sites include: Pelican Marina (PM), Pelican Marina North (PMN), North Buck Island (NBI), Howard Bay (HB), Eagle Ridge (ER), Eagle Ridge South (ERS), Shoalwater Bay (SB) and Agency Lake South (AS). Also shown is Mid-Trench (MDT) where AFA was collected in September, 2011, for use in laboratory experiments.

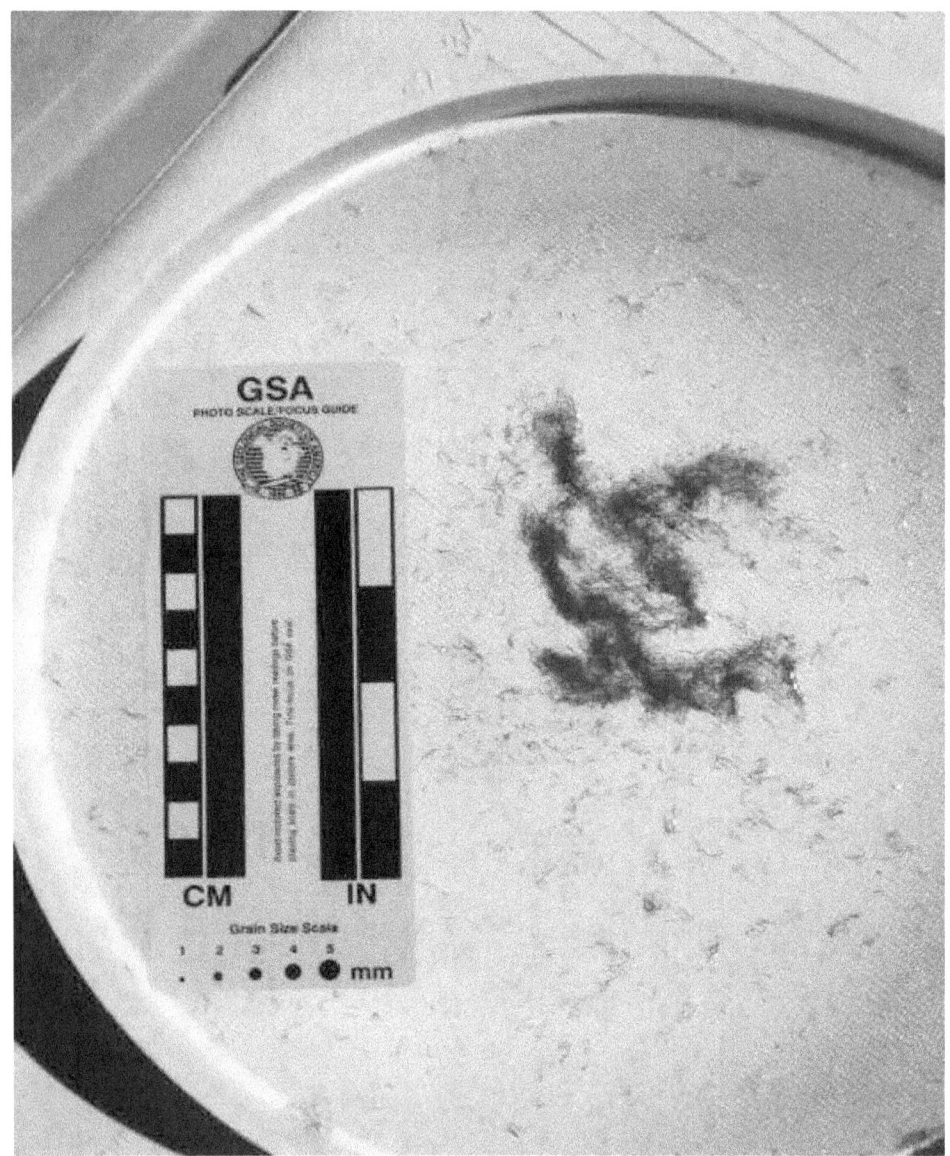

Figure 2. *Aphanizomenon flos-aquae* (AFA) samples were collected using a plastic sieve with a 0.5 millimeter screen. Image is of scant AFA in surface water at North Buck Island on June 29, 2010. There was insufficient AFA to collect a sample.

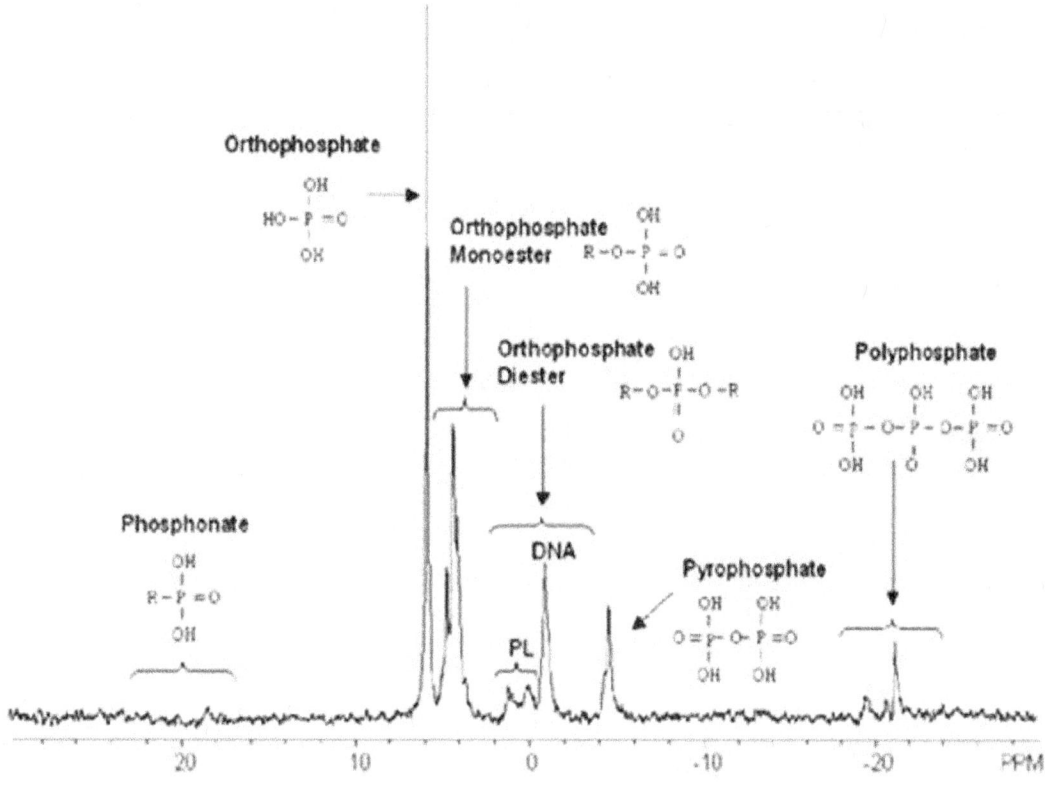

Figure 3. An ideal spectrum of phosphorus-containing compounds. (Figure from Cade-Menum, 2005). The peak at a chemical shift of 7 is orthophosphate. Organic phosphorus compounds range from phosphonates at a chemical shift of 18 to polyphosphates at a chemical shift of -20.

1a 31P NMR

PM - Pelican Marina, AFA collected 7/27/2010, extracted with 0.25M NaOH plus 0.05M EDTA. MDPA added NMR sample in 10M NaOH in D₂0.

Chemical shift values are on the X axis. Chemical shifts of individual peaks are in green. The Y axis indicates the intensity of response.

Bold values in black are peak areas calculated by the TopSpin software.

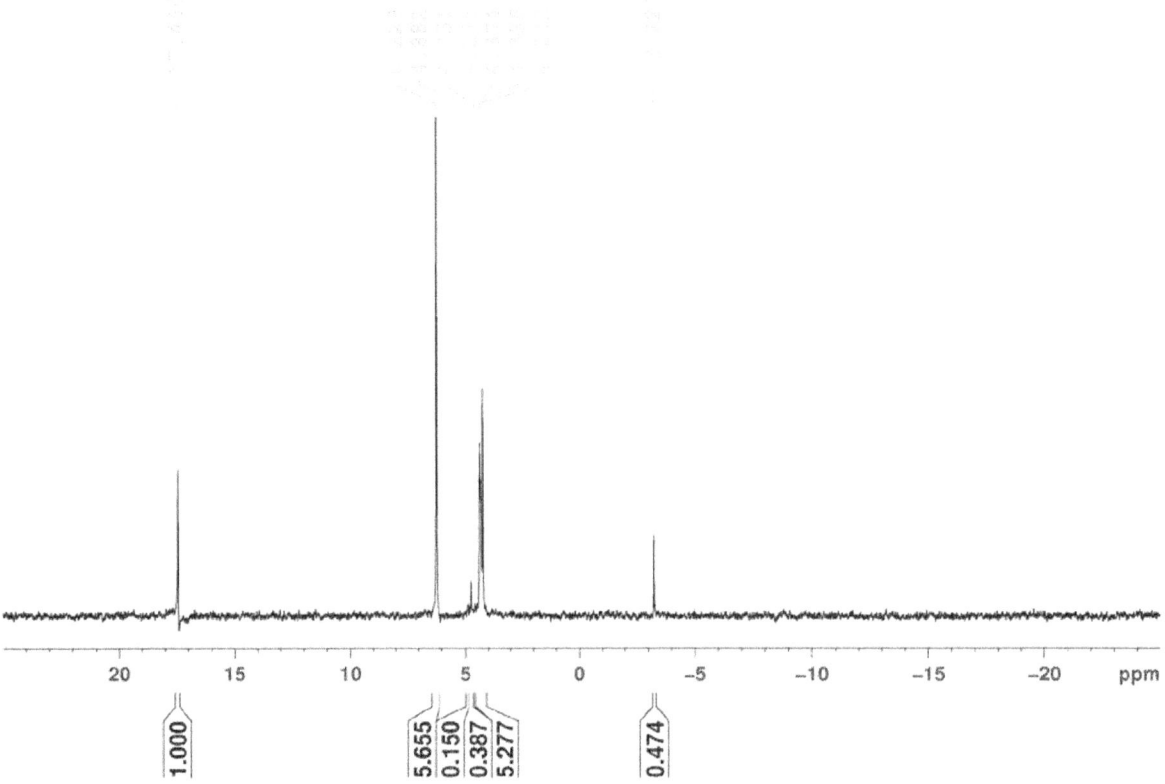

Figure 4. 31P Nuclear Magnetic Resonance data for *Aphanizomenon flos-aquae* (AFA) samples collected in July and August 2010 from Upper Klamath Lake. [P, phosphorus; NMR, Nuclear Magnetic Resonance spectroscopy; AFA, cyanophyte, *Aphanizomenon flos-aquae*; M, molarity, moles per liter of solution; NaOH, sodium hydroxide; EDTA, ethylenediaminetetraacetic acid; MDPA, methylene diphosphonic acid; D₂0, deuterium oxide]

1b. 31P NMR

PM - Pelican Marina, AFA collected 7/27/2010, extracted with water.

No MDPA added. NMR sample in 10M NaOH in D_2O.

Chemical shift values are on the X axis. Chemical shifts of individual peaks are in green.

The Y axis indicates the intensity of response.

Bold values in black are peak areas calculated by the TopSpin software.

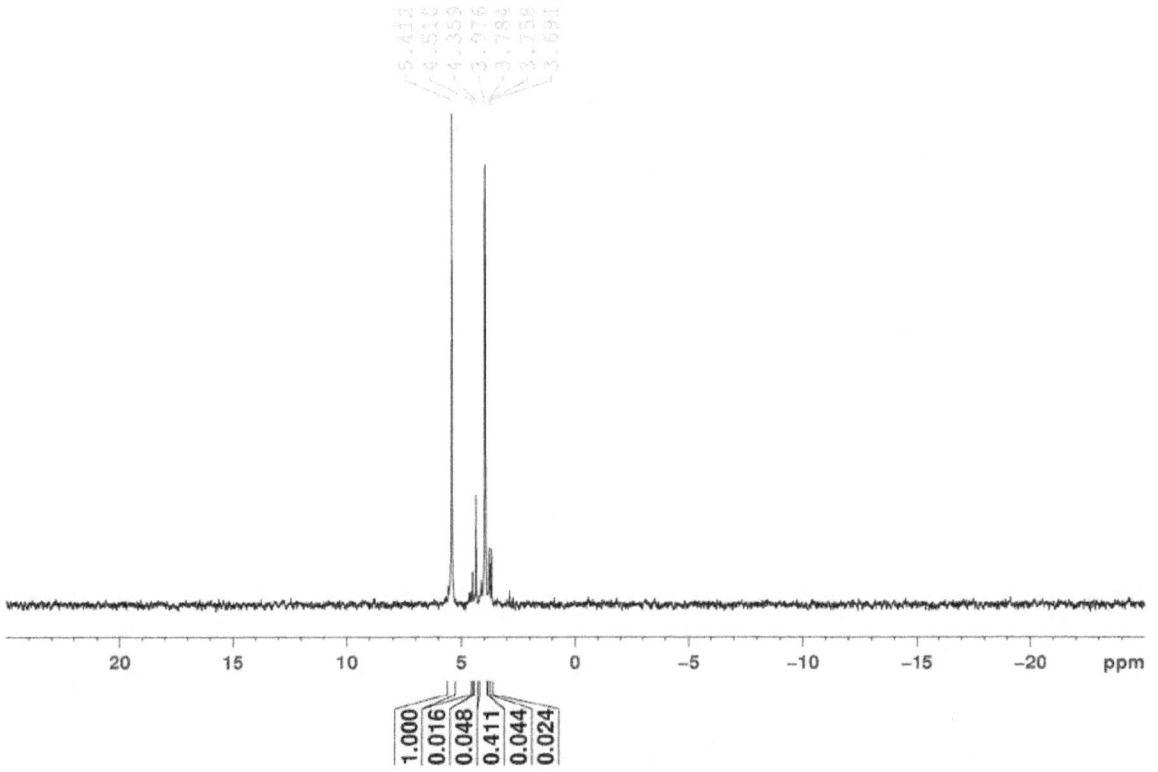

Figure 4. 31P Nuclear Magnetic Resonance data for *Aphanizomenon flos-aquae* (AFA) samples collected in July and August 2010 from Upper Klamath Lake. [P, phosphorus; NMR, Nuclear Magnetic Resonance spectroscopy; AFA, cyanophyte, *Aphanizomenon flos-aquae*; M, molarity, moles per liter of solution; NaOH, sodium hydroxide; EDTA, ethylenediaminetetraacetic acid; MDPA, methylene diphosphonic acid; D_2O, deuterium oxide]—Continued

1c. ³¹P NMR

   PM - Pelican Marina, AFA collected 7/27/2010, extracted with water.

   MDPA added. NMR sample in 10M NaOH in D₂O.

   Chemical shift values are on the X axis. Chemical shifts of individual peaks are in green.
   The Y axis indicates the intensity of response.

   Bold values in black are peak areas calculated by the TopSpin software.

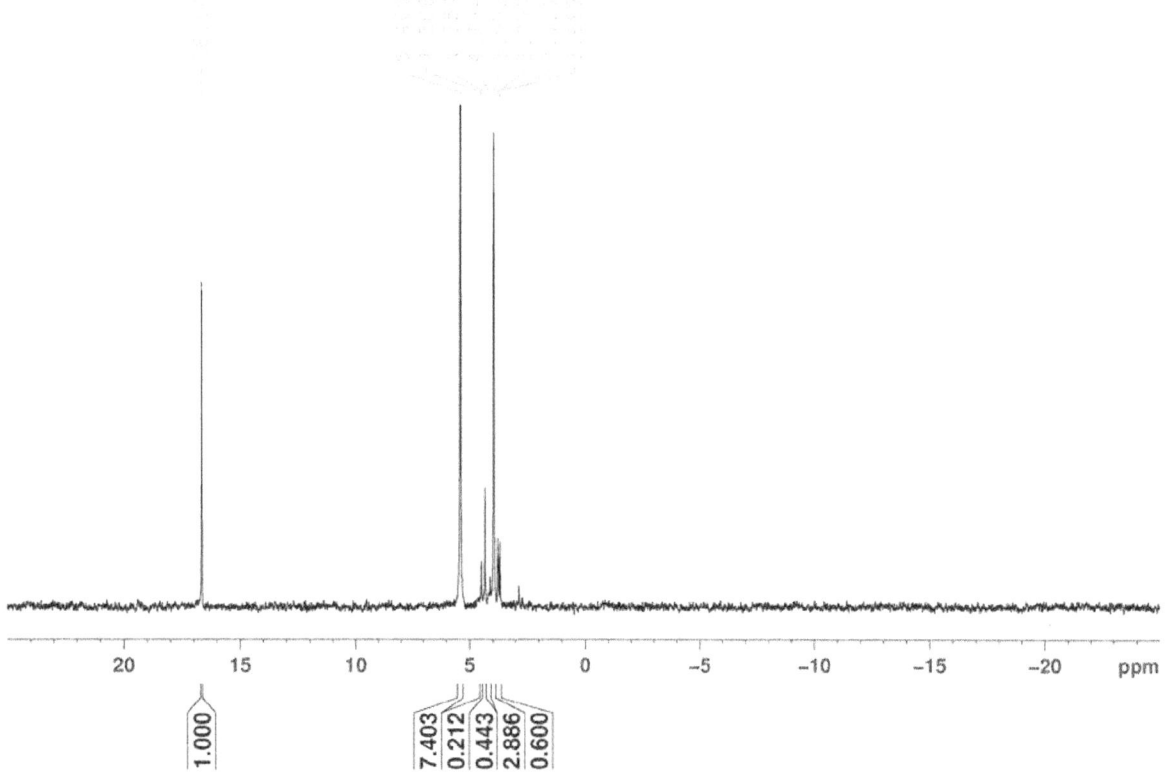

Figure 4. ³¹P Nuclear Magnetic Resonance data for *Aphanizomenon flos-aqua*e (AFA) samples collected in July and August 2010 from Upper Klamath Lake. [P, phosphorus; NMR, Nuclear Magnetic Resonance spectroscopy; AFA, cyanophyte, *Aphanizomenon flos-aquae*; M, molarity, moles per liter of solution; NaOH, sodium hydroxide; EDTA, ethylenediaminetetraacetic acid; MDPA, methylene diphosphonic acid; D₂0, deuterium oxide]—Continued

2a.   31P NMR

   PMN - Pelican Marina North, AFA collected 7/27/2010, extracted with 0.25M NaOH.
   plus 0.05M EDTA. MDPA added. NMR sample in 10M NaOH in D_2O.

   Chemical shift values are on the X axis. Chemical shifts of individual peaks are in green.
   The Y axis indicates the intensity of response.

   Bold values in black are peak areas calculated by the TopSpin software.

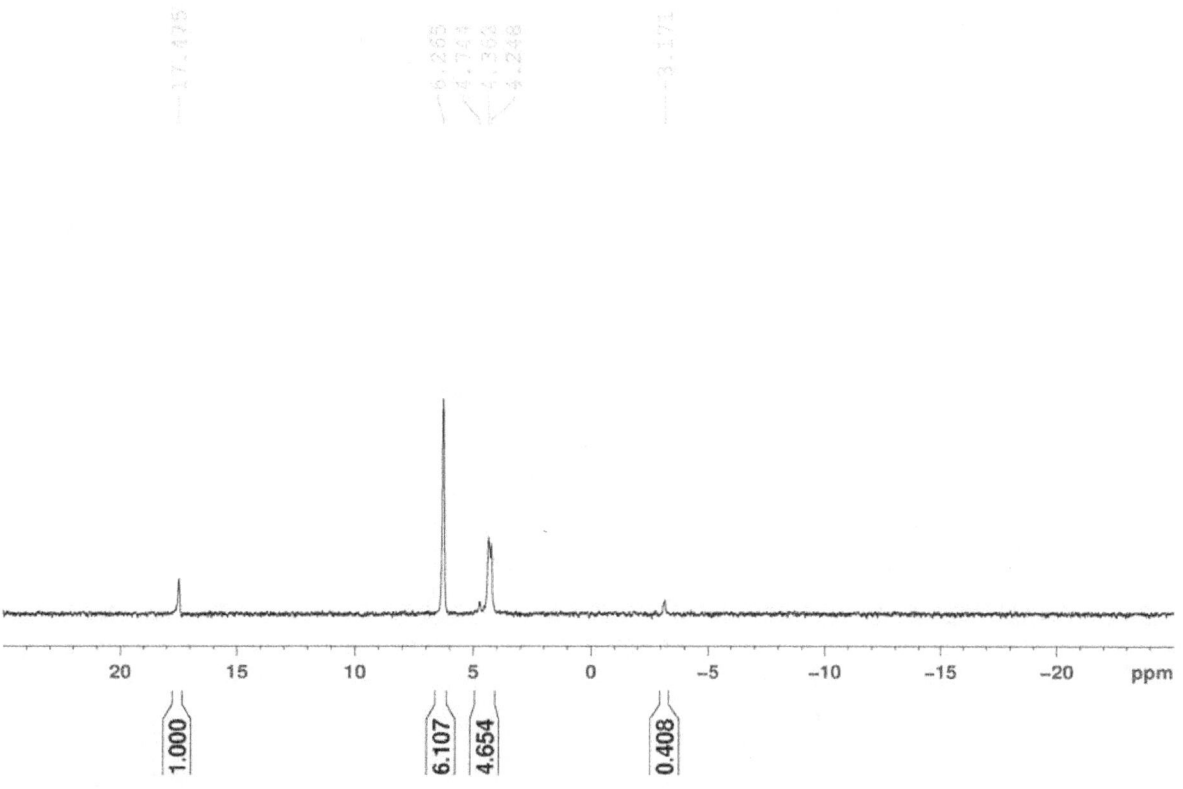

Figure 4.   31P Nuclear Magnetic Resonance data for *Aphanizomenon flos-aquae* (AFA) samples collected in July
and August 2010 from Upper Klamath Lake. [P, phosphorus; NMR, Nuclear Magnetic Resonance spectroscopy;
AFA, cyanophyte, *Aphanizomenon flos-aquae*; M, molarity, moles per liter of solution; NaOH, sodium hydroxide;
EDTA, ethylenediaminetetraacetic acid; MDPA, methylene diphosphonic acid; D_2O, deuterium oxide]—Continued

2b. ^{31}P NMR.

   PMN - Pelican Marina North, AFA collected 7/27/2010, extracted with water only.
   No MDPA added. NMR sample in 10M NaOH in D_2O.

   Chemical shift values are on the X axis. Chemical shifts of individual peaks are in green.
   The Y axis indicates the intensity of response.
   Bold values in black are peak areas calculated by the TopSpin software.

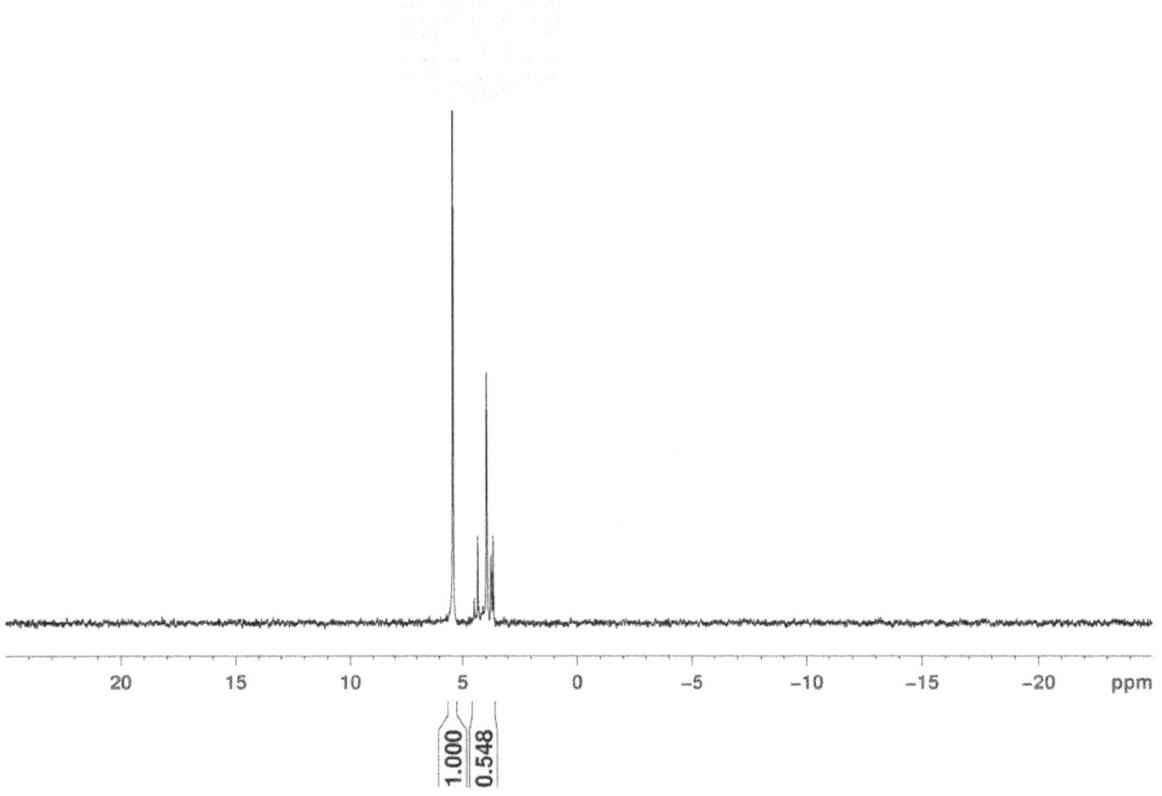

Figure 4. [31]P Nuclear Magnetic Resonance data for *Aphanizomenon flos-aquae* (AFA) samples collected in July and August 2010 from Upper Klamath Lake. [P, phosphorus; NMR, Nuclear Magnetic Resonance spectroscopy; AFA, cyanophyte, *Aphanizomenon flos-aquae*; M, molarity, moles per liter of solution; NaOH, sodium hydroxide; EDTA, ethylenediaminetetraacetic acid; MDPA, methylene diphosphonic acid; D_2O, deuterium oxide]—Continued

2c. ^{31}P NMR.

PMN - Pelican Marina North, AFA collected 7/27/2010, extracted with water.
MDPA added. NMR sample in 10M NaOH in D$_2$O.

Chemical shift values are on the X axis. Chemical shifts of individual peaks are in green.
The Y axis indicates the intensity of response.

Bold values in black are peak areas calculated by the TopSpin software.

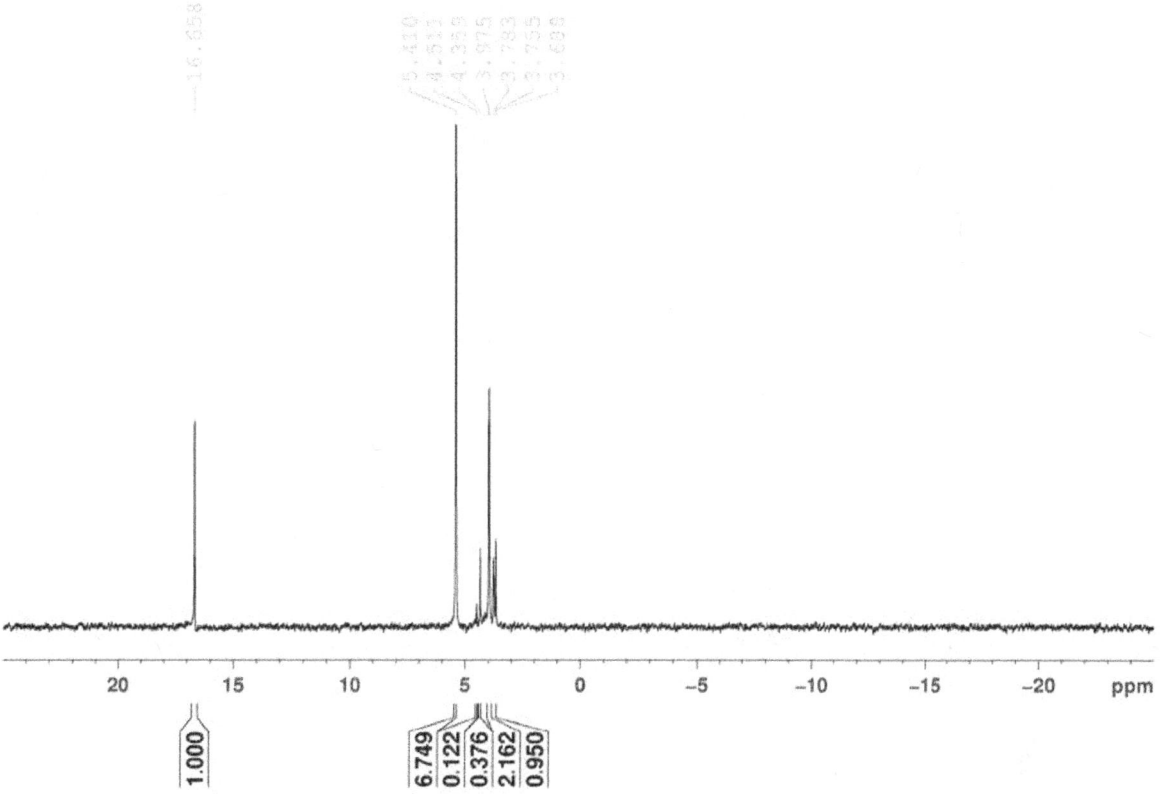

Figure 4. ^{31}P Nuclear Magnetic Resonance data for *Aphanizomenon flos-aquae* (AFA) samples collected in July and August 2010 from Upper Klamath Lake. [P, phosphorus; NMR, Nuclear Magnetic Resonance spectroscopy; AFA, cyanophyte, *Aphanizomenon flos-aquae*; M, molarity, moles per liter of solution; NaOH, sodium hydroxide; EDTA, ethylenediaminetetraacetic acid; MDPA, methylene diphosphonic acid; D$_2$0, deuterium oxide]—Continued

3a. ^{31}P NMR

   PM - Pelican Marina, AFA collected 8/9/2010, extracted with 0.25M NaOH
   plus 0.05M EDTA. MDPA added. NMR sample in 10M NaOH in D$_2$O.

   Chemical shift values are on the X axis. Chemical shifts of individual peaks are in green.
   The Y axis indicates the intensity of response.

   Bold values in black are peak areas calculated by the TopSpin software.

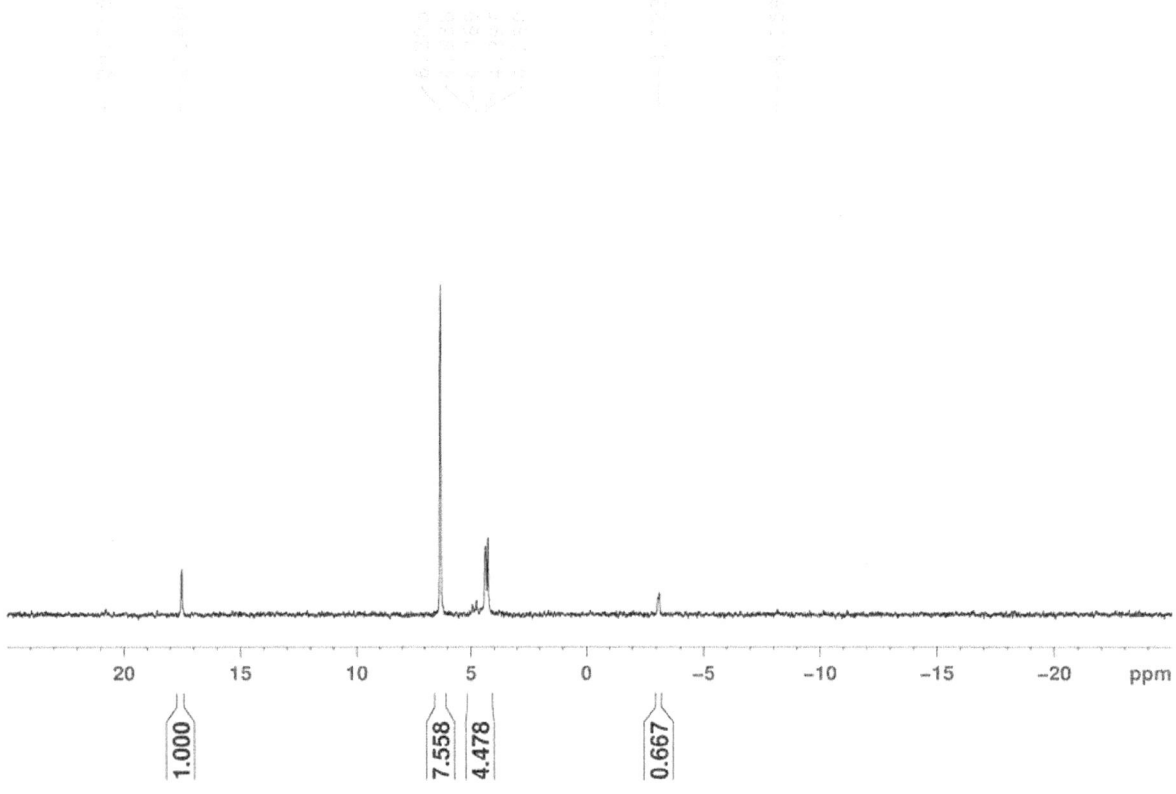

Figure 4. ^{31}P Nuclear Magnetic Resonance data for *Aphanizomenon flos-aqua*e (AFA) samples collected in July and August 2010 from Upper Klamath Lake. [P, phosphorus; NMR, Nuclear Magnetic Resonance spectroscopy; AFA, cyanophyte, *Aphanizomenon flos-aquae*; M, molarity, moles per liter of solution; NaOH, sodium hydroxide; EDTA, ethylenediaminetetraacetic acid; MDPA, methylene diphosphonic acid; D$_2$0, deuterium oxide]—Continued

3b. ^{31}P NMR

PM - Pelican Marina, AFA collected 8/9/2010, extracted with water.
No MDPA added. NMR sample in 10M NaOH in D^{2}O.
Chemical shift values are on the X axis. Chemical shifts of individual peaks are in green.
The Y axis indicates the intensity of response.
Bold values in black are peak areas calculated by the TopSpin software.

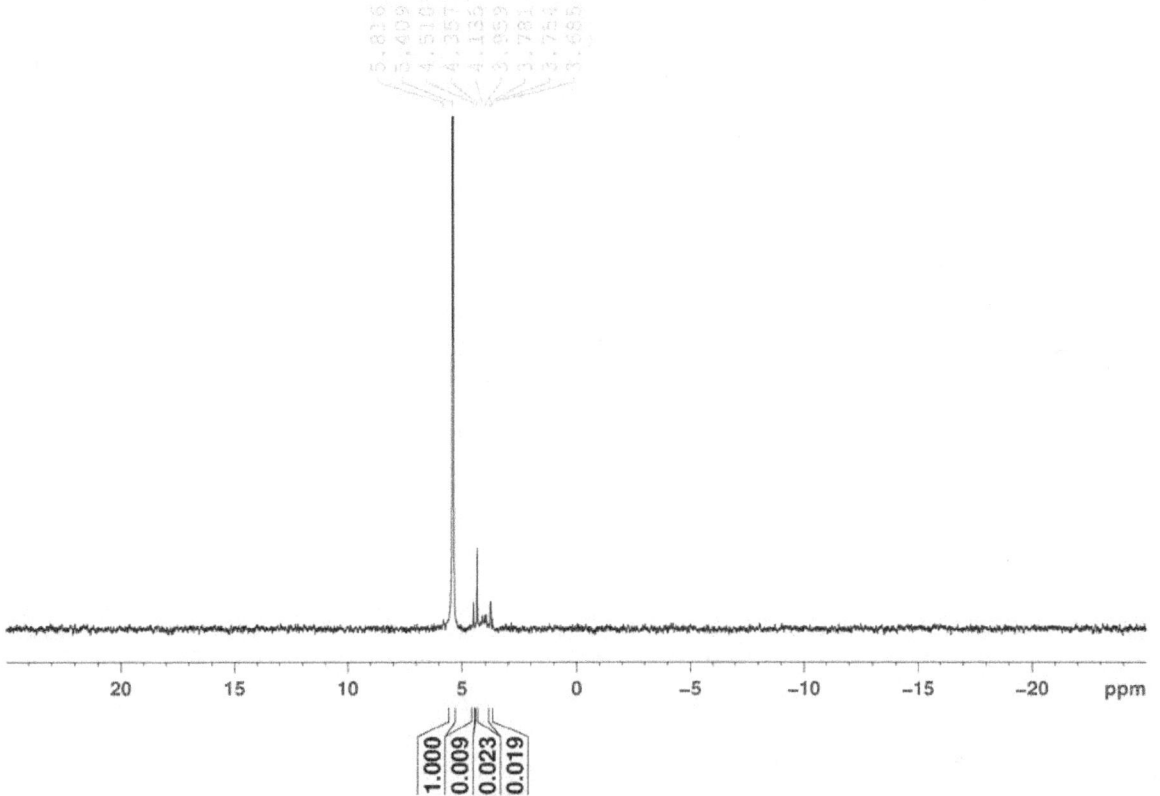

Figure 4. ^{31}P Nuclear Magnetic Resonance data for *Aphanizomenon flos-aquae* (AFA) samples collected in July and August 2010 from Upper Klamath Lake. [P, phosphorus; NMR, Nuclear Magnetic Resonance spectroscopy; AFA, cyanophyte, *Aphanizomenon flos-aquae*; M, molarity, moles per liter of solution; NaOH, sodium hydroxide; EDTA, ethylenediaminetetraacetic acid; MDPA, methylene diphosphonic acid; D$_2$0, deuterium oxide]—Continued

3c. ^{31}P NMR

   PM - Pelican Marina, AFA collected 8/9/2010, extracted with water.
   MDPA added. NMR sample in 10M NaOH in D_2O.
   Chemical shift values are on the X axis. Chemical shifts of individual peaks are in green.
   The Y axis indicates the intensity of response.
   Bold values in black are peak areas calculated by the TopSpin software.

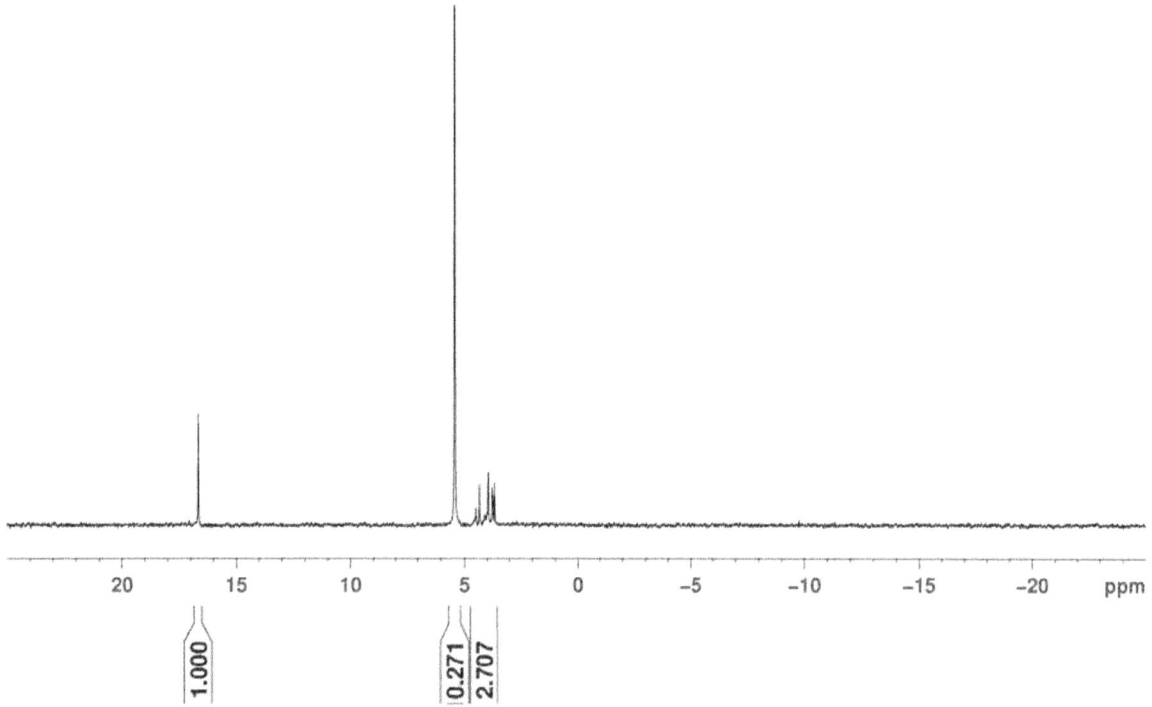

Figure 4. ^{31}P Nuclear Magnetic Resonance data for *Aphanizomenon flos-aquae* (AFA) samples collected in July and August 2010 from Upper Klamath Lake. [P, phosphorus; NMR, Nuclear Magnetic Resonance spectroscopy; AFA, cyanophyte, *Aphanizomenon flos-aquae*; M, molarity, moles per liter of solution; NaOH, sodium hydroxide; EDTA, ethylenediaminetetraacetic acid; MDPA, methylene diphosphonic acid; D_2O, deuterium oxide]—Continued

4a. ^{31}P NMR

NBI - North Buck Island, AFA collected 7/27/2010, extracted with 0.25M NaOH.
plus 0.05M EDTA. MDPA added. NMR sample in 10M NaOH in D_2O.
Chemical shift values are on the X axis. Chemical shifts of individual peaks are in green.
The Y axis indicates the intensity of response.
Bold values in black are peak areas calculated by the TopSpin software.

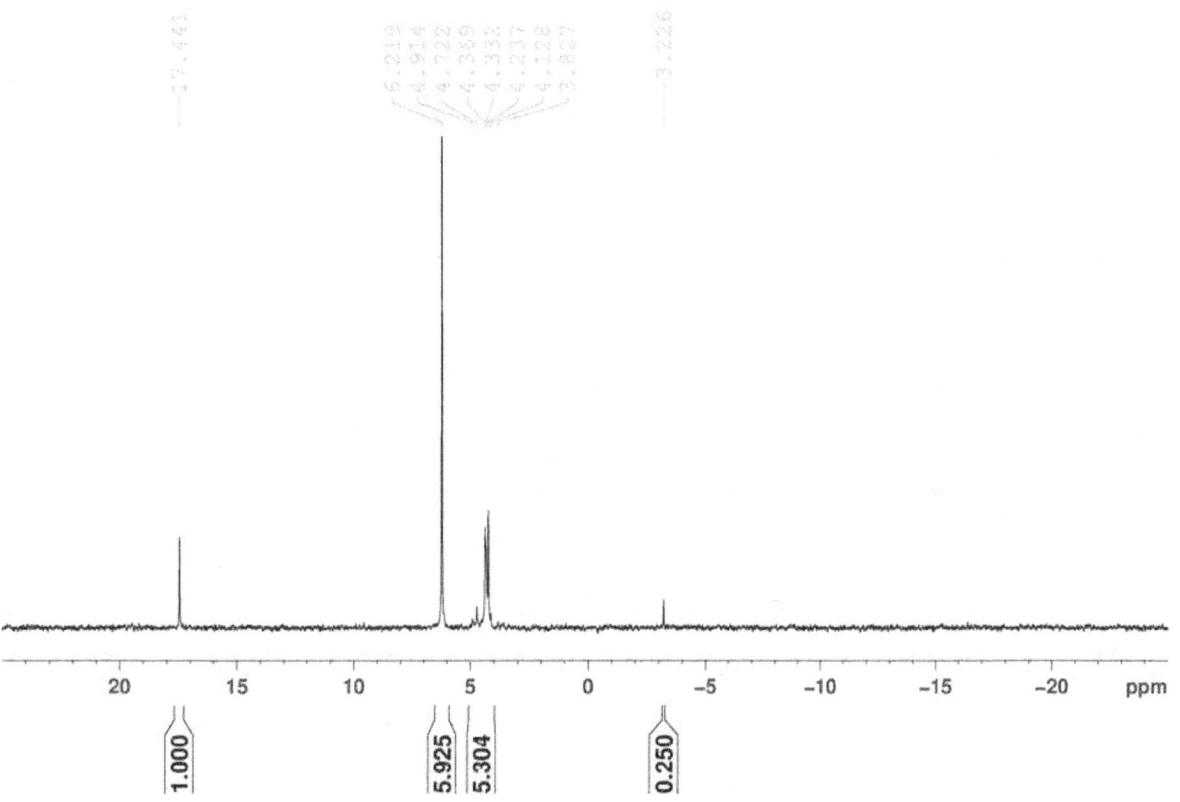

Figure 4. ^{31}P Nuclear Magnetic Resonance data for *Aphanizomenon flos-aquae* (AFA) samples collected in July and August 2010 from Upper Klamath Lake. [P, phosphorus; NMR, Nuclear Magnetic Resonance spectroscopy; AFA, cyanophyte, *Aphanizomenon flos-aquae*; M, molarity, moles per liter of solution; NaOH, sodium hydroxide; EDTA, ethylenediaminetetraacetic acid; MDPA, methylene diphosphonic acid; D_2O, deuterium oxide]—Continued

4b. ^{31}P NMR

NBI - North Buck Island, AFA collected 7/27/2010, extracted with water.

No MDPA added. NMR sample in 10M NaOH in D_2O. On the X axis are chemical shift values.

Chemical shift values are on the X axis. Chemical shifts of individual peaks are in green.

The Y axis indicates the intensity of response.

Bold values in black are peak areas calculated by the TopSpin software.

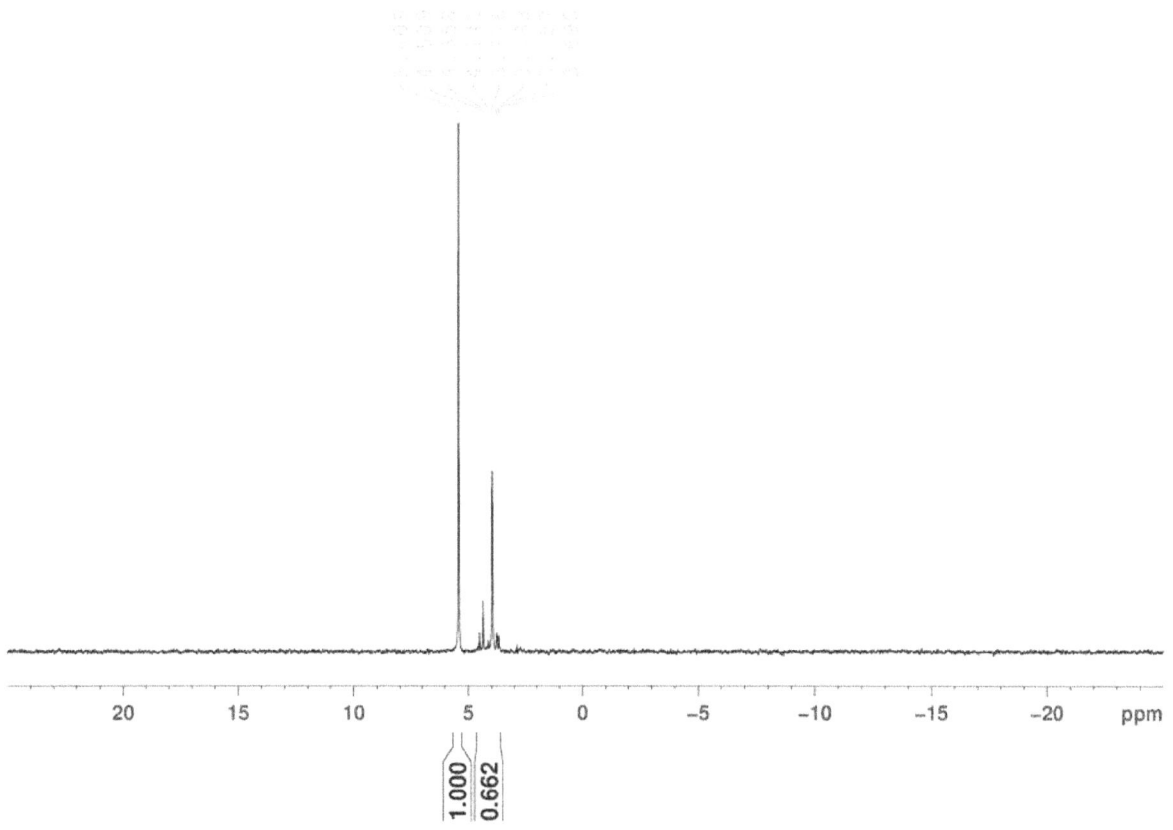

Figure 4. ^{31}P Nuclear Magnetic Resonance data for *Aphanizomenon flos-aqua*e (AFA) samples collected in July and August 2010 from Upper Klamath Lake. [P, phosphorus; NMR, Nuclear Magnetic Resonance spectroscopy; AFA, cyanophyte, *Aphanizomenon flos-aquae*; M, molarity, moles per liter of solution; NaOH, sodium hydroxide; EDTA, ethylenediaminetetraacetic acid; MDPA, methylene diphosphonic acid; D_2O, deuterium oxide]—Continued

4c. ^{31}P NMR

NBI - North Buck Island, AFA collected 7/27/2010, extracted with water.

MDPA added. NMR sample in 10M NaOH in D$_2$O.

Chemical shift values are on the X axis. Chemical shifts of individual peaks are in green.

The Y axis indicates the intensity of response.

Bold values in black are peak areas calculated by the TopSpin software.

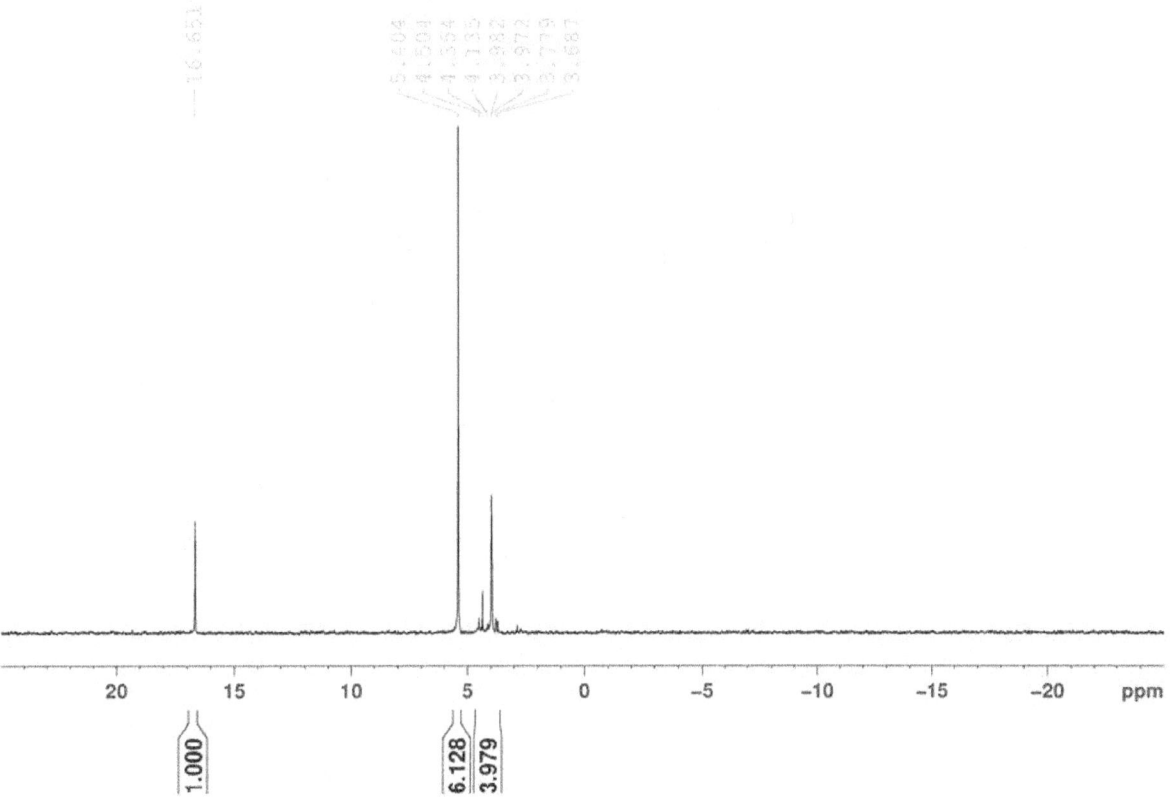

Figure 4. ^{31}P Nuclear Magnetic Resonance data for *Aphanizomenon flos-aquae* (AFA) samples collected in July and August 2010 from Upper Klamath Lake. [P, phosphorus; NMR, Nuclear Magnetic Resonance spectroscopy; AFA, cyanophyte, *Aphanizomenon flos-aquae*; M, molarity, moles per liter of solution; NaOH, sodium hydroxide; EDTA, ethylenediaminetetraacetic acid; MDPA, methylene diphosphonic acid; D$_2$0, deuterium oxide]—Continued

5a. ^{31}P NMR

HB - Howard Bay AFA collected 8/9/2010, extracted with 0.25M NaOH.
plus 0.05M EDTA. MDPA added. NMR sample in 10M NaOH in D$_2$O.
Chemical shift values are on the X axis. Chemical shifts of individual peaks are in green.
The Y axis indicates the intensity of response. Bold values in black are peak areas calculated by
the TopSpin software.

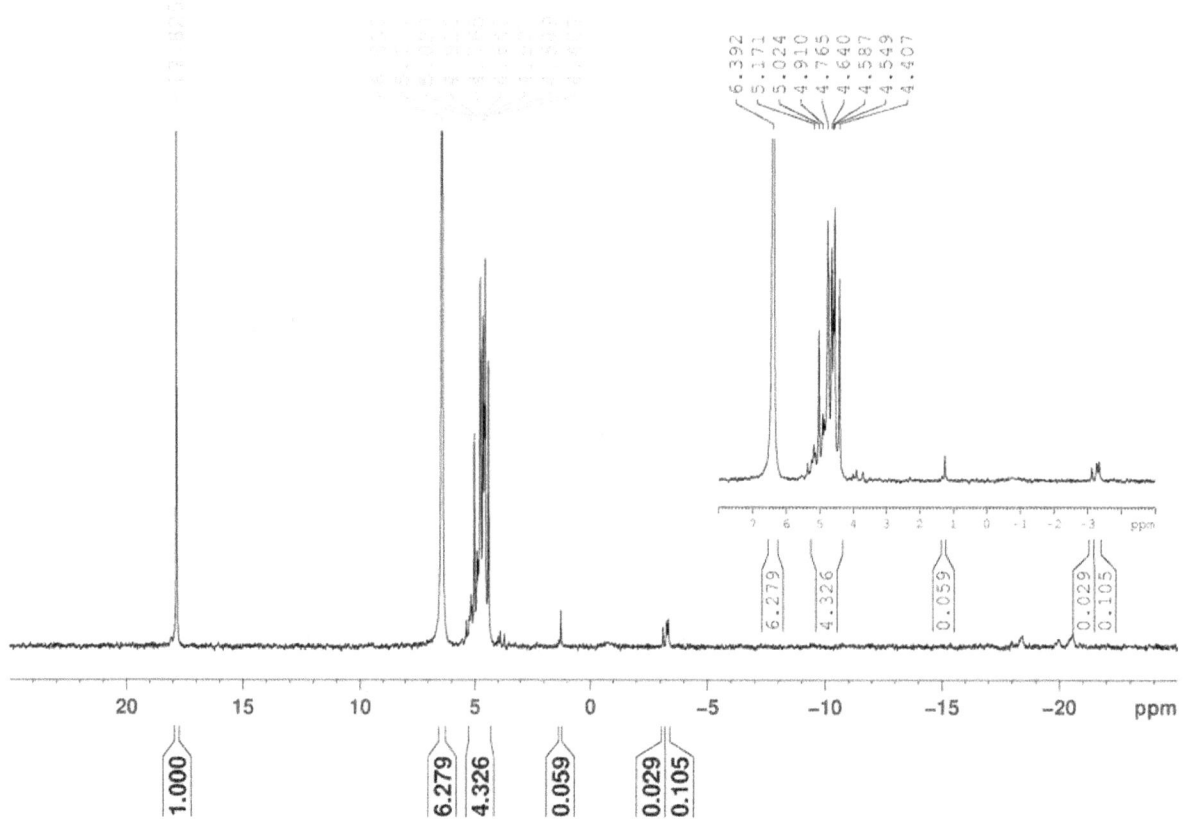

Figure 4. ^{31}P Nuclear Magnetic Resonance data for *Aphanizomenon flos-aqua*e (AFA) samples collected in July and August 2010 from Upper Klamath Lake. [P, phosphorus; NMR, Nuclear Magnetic Resonance spectroscopy; AFA, cyanophyte, *Aphanizomenon flos-aquae*; M, molarity, moles per liter of solution; NaOH, sodium hydroxide; EDTA, ethylenediaminetetraacetic acid; MDPA, methylene diphosphonic acid; D$_2$0, deuterium oxide]—Continued

5b. ^{31}P NMR

HB - Howard Bay AFA collected 8/9/2010, extracted with water.
No MDPA added. NMR sample in 10M NaOH in D_2O.
Chemical shift values are on the X axis. Chemical shifts of individual peaks are in green.
The Y axis indicates the intensity of response.
Bold values in black are peak areas calculated by the TopSpin software.

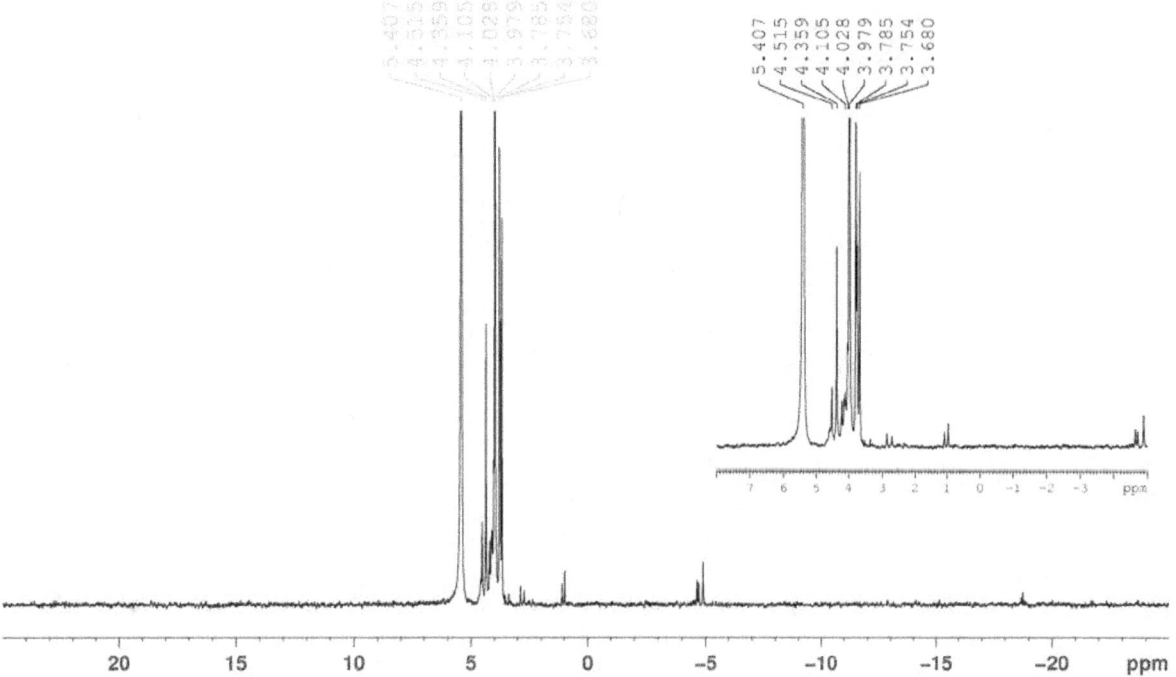

Figure 4. ^{31}P Nuclear Magnetic Resonance data for *Aphanizomenon flos-aquae* (AFA) samples collected in July and August 2010 from Upper Klamath Lake. [P, phosphorus; NMR, Nuclear Magnetic Resonance spectroscopy; AFA, cyanophyte, *Aphanizomenon flos-aquae*; M, molarity, moles per liter of solution; NaOH, sodium hydroxide; EDTA, ethylenediaminetetraacetic acid; MDPA, methylene diphosphonic acid; D_2O, deuterium oxide]—Continued

5c. ^{31}P NMR

HB - Howard Bay AFA collected 8/9/2010, extracted with water.

MDPA added. NMR sample in 10M NaOH in D$_2$O.

Chemical shift values are on the X axis. Chemical shifts of individual peaks are in green.

The Y axis indicates the intensity of response.

Bold values in black are peak areas calculated by the TopSpin software.

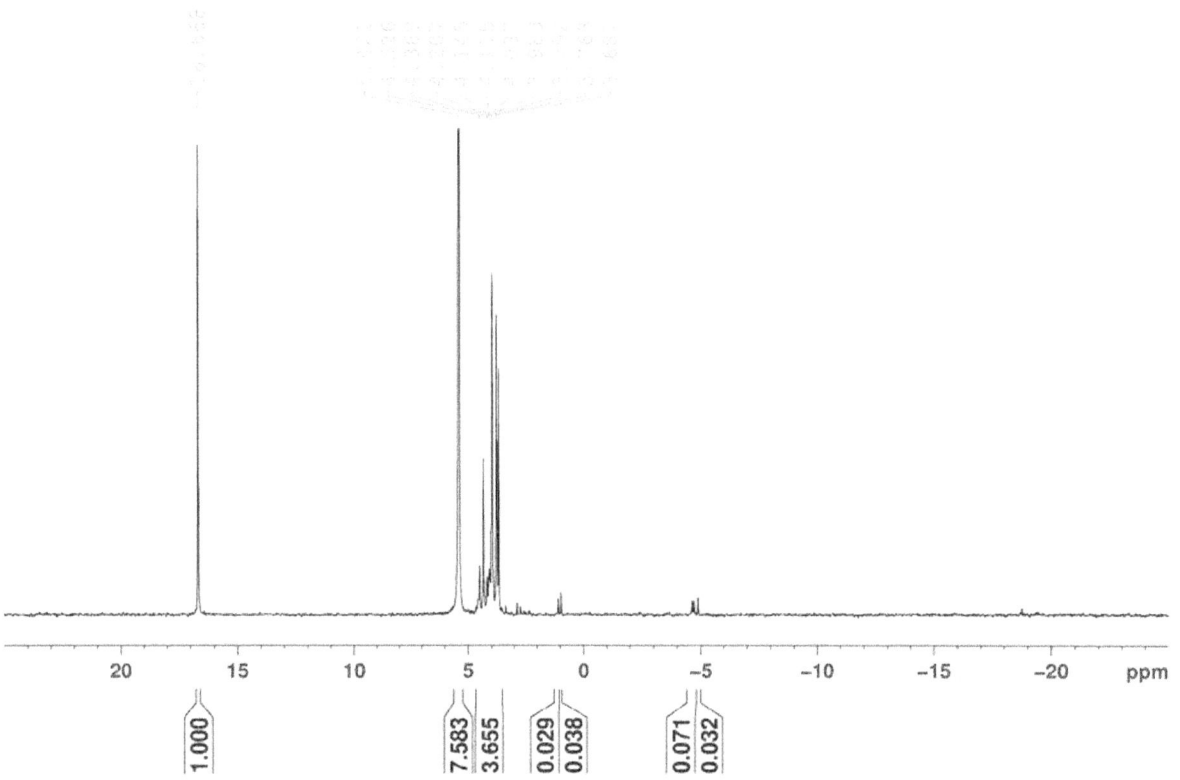

Figure 4. ^{31}P Nuclear Magnetic Resonance data for *Aphanizomenon flos-aquae* (AFA) samples collected in July and August 2010 from Upper Klamath Lake. [P, phosphorus; NMR, Nuclear Magnetic Resonance spectroscopy; AFA, cyanophyte, *Aphanizomenon flos-aquae*; M, molarity, moles per liter of solution; NaOH, sodium hydroxide; EDTA, ethylenediaminetetraacetic acid; MDPA, methylene diphosphonic acid; D$_2$0, deuterium oxide]—Continued

6a. ^{31}P NMR

ER - Eagle Ridge, AFA collected 8/9/2010, extracted with 0.25M NaOH.
plus 0.05M EDTA. MDPA added. NMR sample in 10M NaOH in D$_2$O.
Chemical shift values are on the X axis. Chemical shifts of individual peaks are in green.
The Y axis indicates the intensity of response.
Bold values in black are peak areas calculated by the TopSpin software.

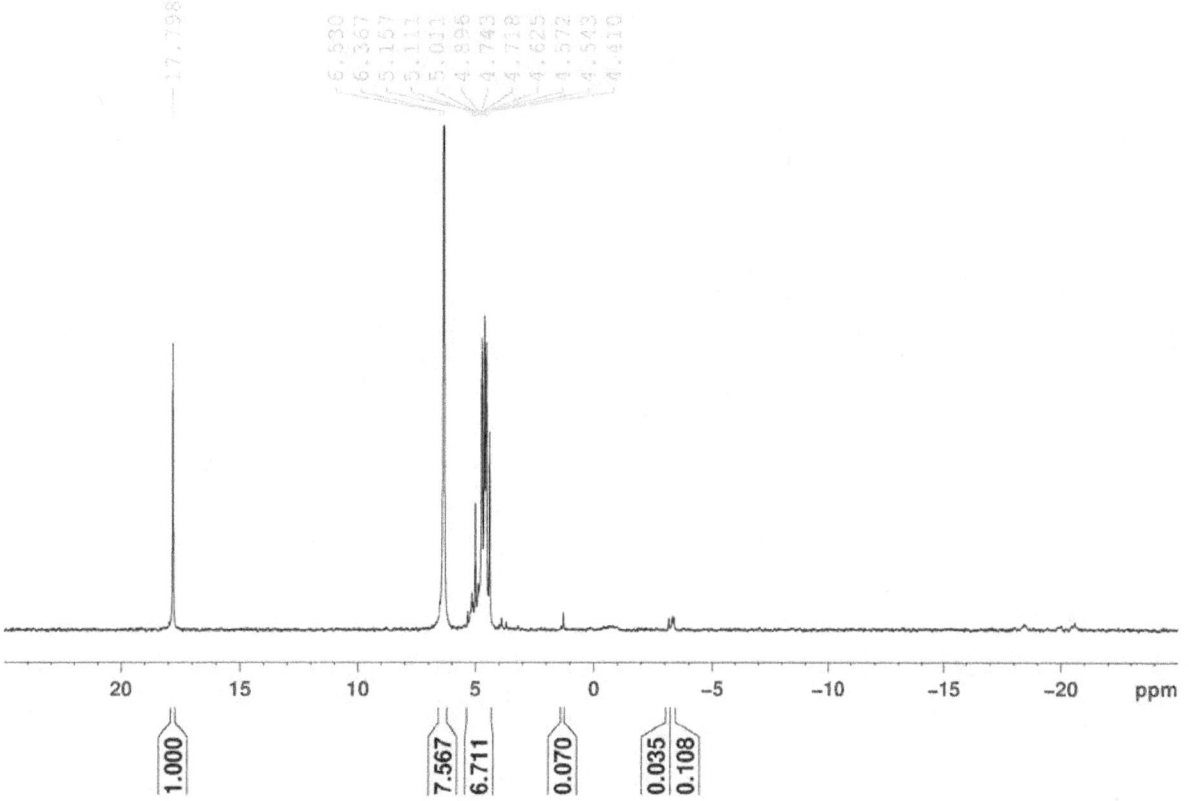

Figure 4. ^{31}P Nuclear Magnetic Resonance data for *Aphanizomenon flos-aquae* (AFA) samples collected in July and August 2010 from Upper Klamath Lake. [P, phosphorus; NMR, Nuclear Magnetic Resonance spectroscopy; AFA, cyanophyte, *Aphanizomenon flos-aquae*; M, molarity, moles per liter of solution; NaOH, sodium hydroxide; EDTA, ethylenediaminetetraacetic acid; MDPA, methylene diphosphonic acid; D$_2$0, deuterium oxide]—Continued

6b. ^{31}P NMR

ER - Eagle Ridge, AFA collected 8/9/2010, extracted with water.
No MDPA added. NMR sample in 10M NaOH in D$_2$O.
Chemical shift values are on the X axis. Chemical shifts of individual peaks are in green.
The Y axis indicates the intensity of response.
Bold values in black are peak areas calculated by the TopSpin software.

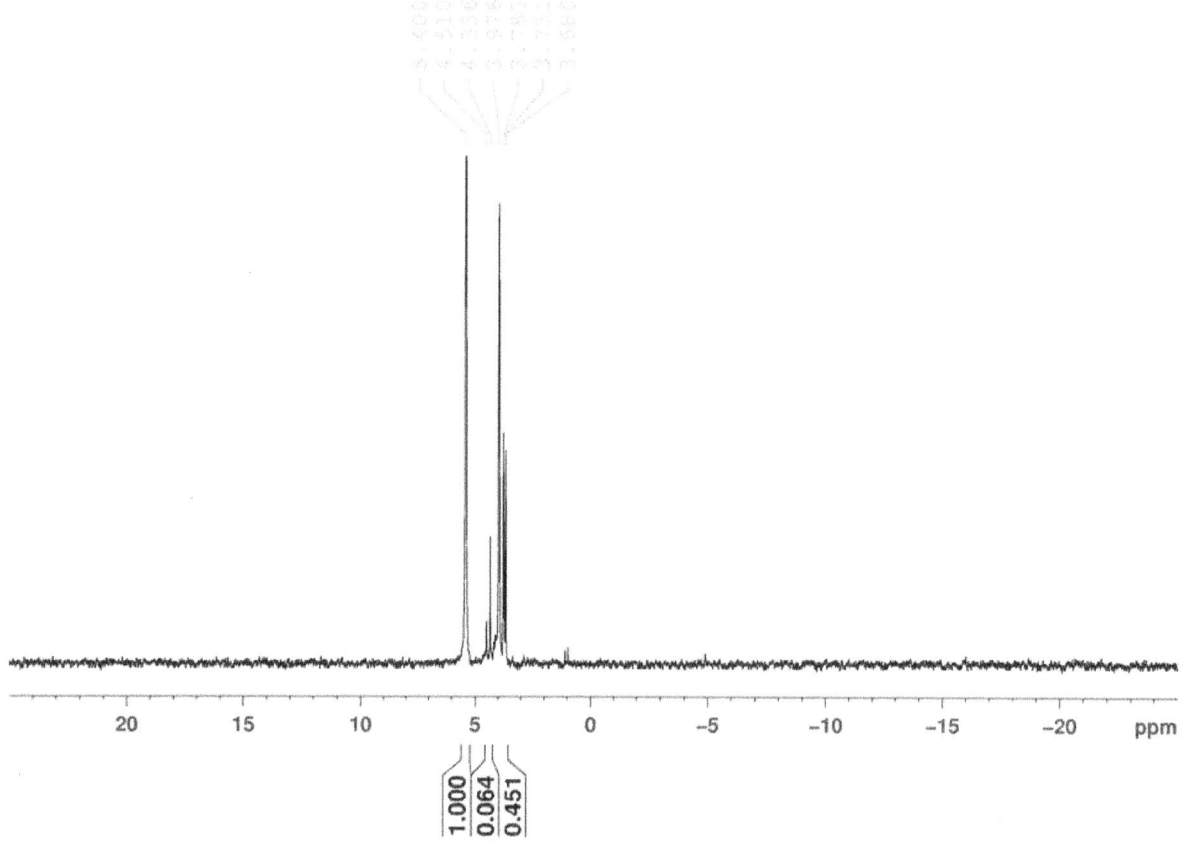

Figure 4. ^{31}P Nuclear Magnetic Resonance data for *Aphanizomenon flos-aqua*e (AFA) samples collected in July and August 2010 from Upper Klamath Lake. [P, phosphorus; NMR, Nuclear Magnetic Resonance spectroscopy; AFA, cyanophyte, *Aphanizomenon flos-aquae*; M, molarity, moles per liter of solution; NaOH, sodium hydroxide; EDTA, ethylenediaminetetraacetic acid; MDPA, methylene diphosphonic acid; D$_2$0, deuterium oxide]—Continued

6c. ^{31}P NMR

ER - Eagle Ridge, AFA collected 8/9/2010, extracted with water.

MDPA added. NMR sample in 10M NaOH in D_2O.

Chemical shift values are on the X axis. Chemical shifts of individual peaks are in green.

The Y axis indicates the intensity of response.

Bold values in black are peak areas calculated by the TopSpin software.

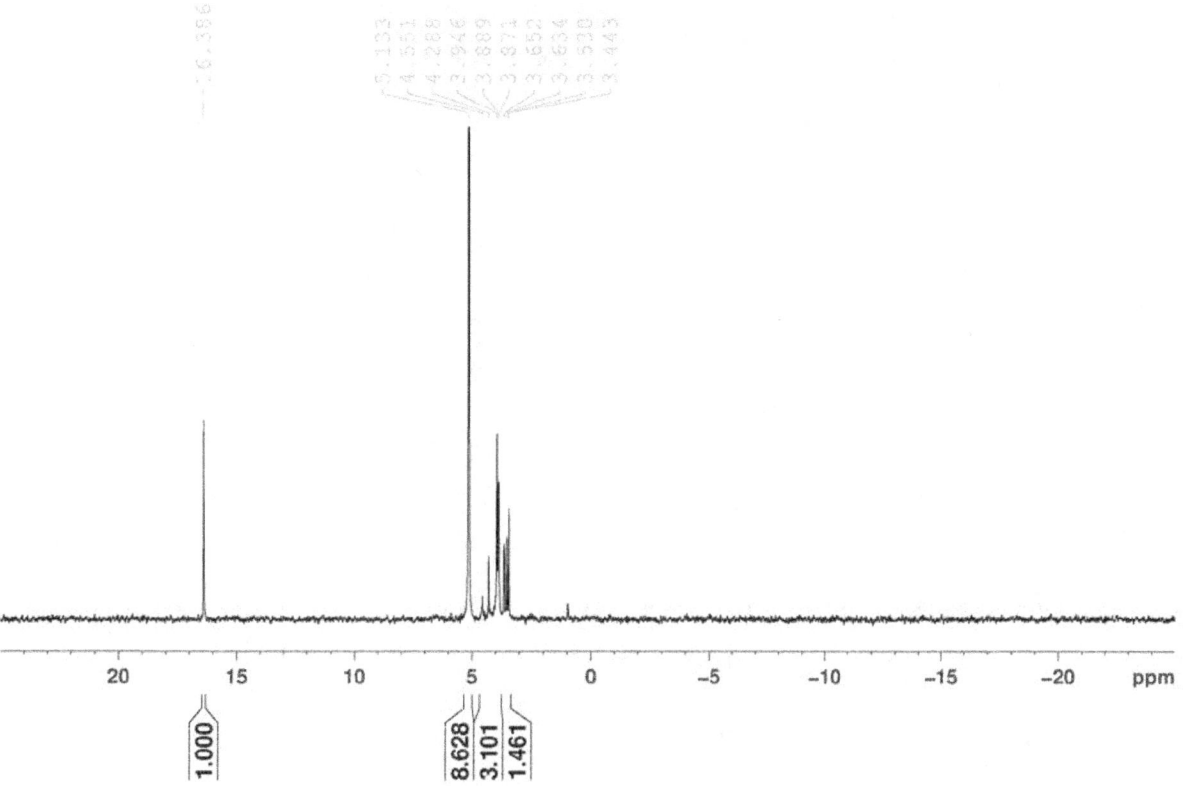

Figure 4. ^{31}P Nuclear Magnetic Resonance data for *Aphanizomenon flos-aquae* (AFA) samples collected in July and August 2010 from Upper Klamath Lake. [P, phosphorus; NMR, Nuclear Magnetic Resonance spectroscopy; AFA, cyanophyte, *Aphanizomenon flos-aquae*; M, molarity, moles per liter of solution; NaOH, sodium hydroxide; EDTA, ethylenediaminetetraacetic acid; MDPA, methylene diphosphonic acid; D_2O, deuterium oxide]—Continued

7a. ^{31}P NMR

ERS - Eagle Ridge South, AFA collected 8/12/2010, extracted with 0.25M NaOH.
plus 0.05M EDTA. MDPA added. NMR sample in 10M NaOH in D$_2$O.
Chemical shift values are on the X axis. Chemical shifts of individual peaks are in green.
The Y axis indicates the intensity of response.
Bold values in black are peak areas calculated by the TopSpin software.

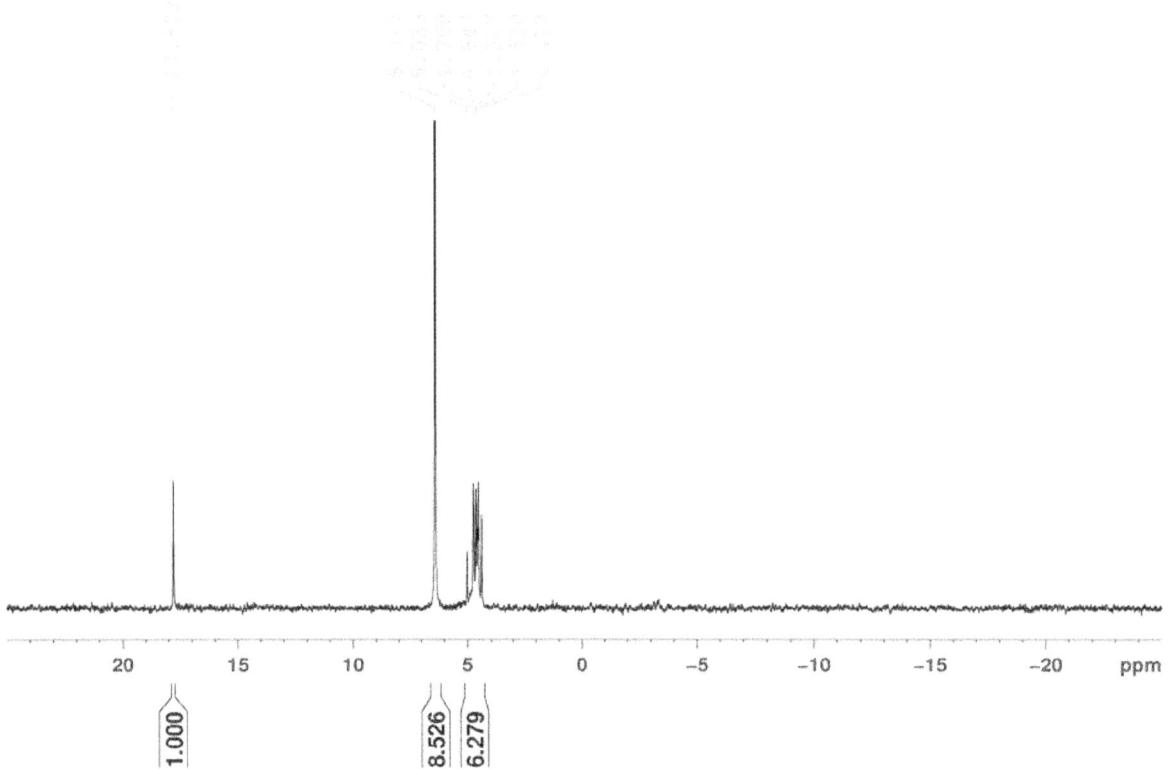

Figure 4. ^{31}P Nuclear Magnetic Resonance data for *Aphanizomenon flos-aqua*e (AFA) samples collected in July and August 2010 from Upper Klamath Lake. [P, phosphorus; NMR, Nuclear Magnetic Resonance spectroscopy; AFA, cyanophyte, *Aphanizomenon flos-aquae*; M, molarity, moles per liter of solution; NaOH, sodium hydroxide; EDTA, ethylenediaminetetraacetic acid; MDPA, methylene diphosphonic acid; D$_2$0, deuterium oxide]—Continued

7b. ^{31}P NMR

ERS - Eagle Ridge South, AFA collected 8/12/2010, extracted with water.

No MDPA added. NMR sample in 10M NaOH in D_2O.

Chemical shift values are on the X axis. Chemical shifts of individual peaks are in green.

The Y axis indicates the intensity of response.

Bold values in black are peak areas calculated by the TopSpin software.

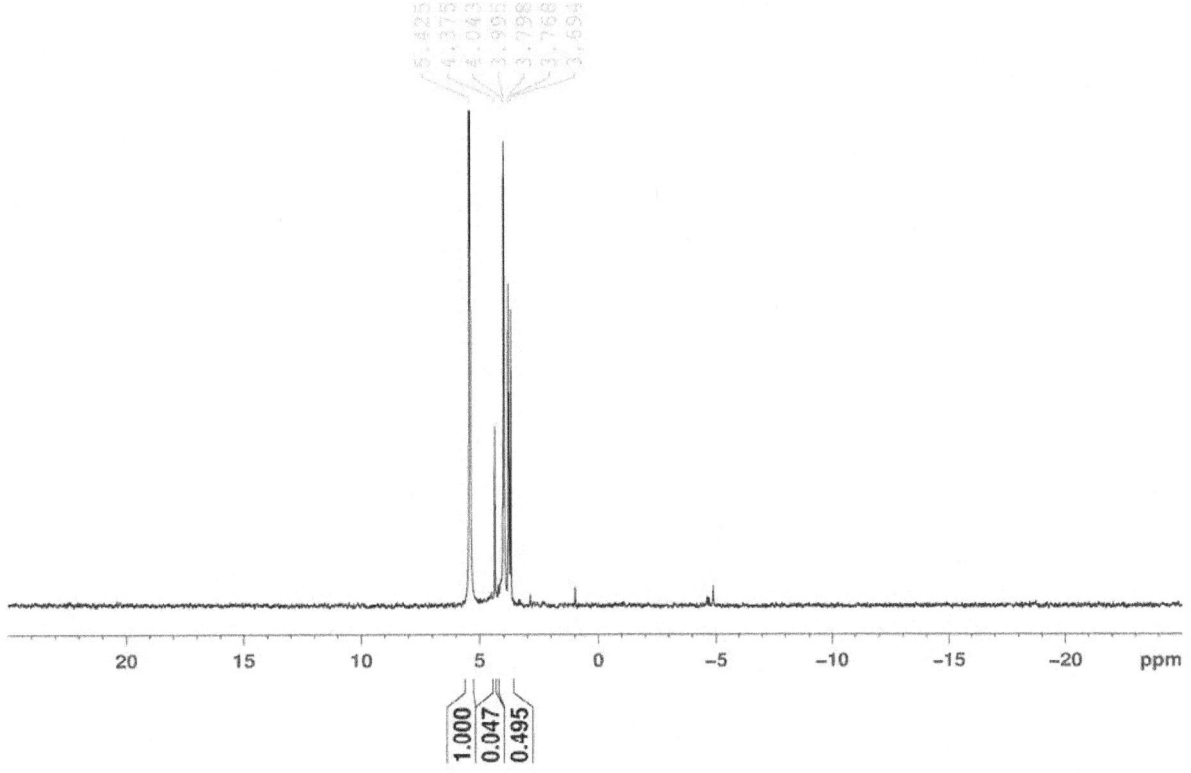

Figure 4. ^{31}P Nuclear Magnetic Resonance data for *Aphanizomenon flos-aquae* (AFA) samples collected in July and August 2010 from Upper Klamath Lake. [P, phosphorus; NMR, Nuclear Magnetic Resonance spectroscopy; AFA, cyanophyte, *Aphanizomenon flos-aquae*; M, molarity, moles per liter of solution; NaOH, sodium hydroxide; EDTA, ethylenediaminetetraacetic acid; MDPA, methylene diphosphonic acid; D_2O, deuterium oxide]—Continued

7c. ^{31}P NMR

ERS - Eagle Ridge South, AFA collected 8/12/2010, extracted with water.
MDPA added. NMR sample in 10M NaOH in D$_2$O.
Chemical shift values are on the X axis. Chemical shifts of individual peaks are in green.
The Y axis indicates the intensity of response.
Bold values in black are peak areas calculated by the TopSpin software.

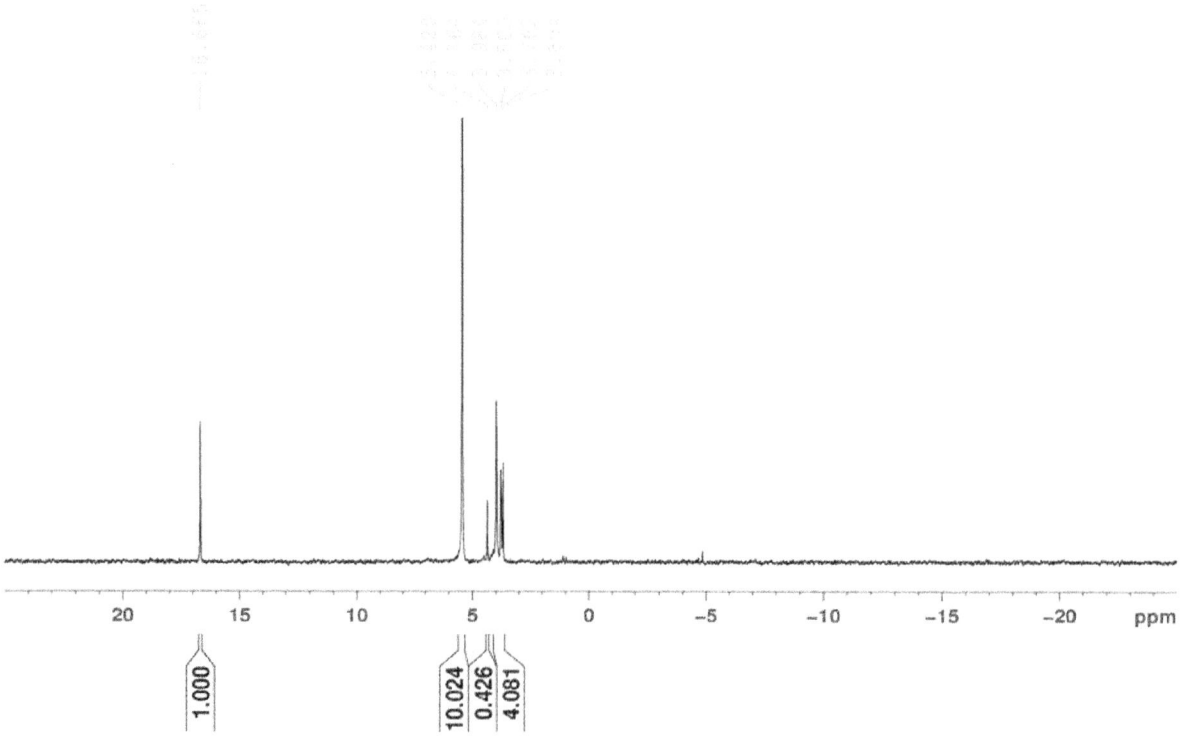

Figure 4. ^{31}P Nuclear Magnetic Resonance data for *Aphanizomenon flos-aqua*e (AFA) samples collected in July and August 2010 from Upper Klamath Lake. [P, phosphorus; NMR, Nuclear Magnetic Resonance spectroscopy; AFA, cyanophyte, *Aphanizomenon flos-aquae*; M, molarity, moles per liter of solution; NaOH, sodium hydroxide; EDTA, ethylenediaminetetraacetic acid; MDPA, methylene diphosphonic acid; D$_2$0, deuterium oxide]—Continued

8a. ^{31}P NMR

SB - Shoalwater Bay, AFA collected 8/9/2010, extracted with 0.25M NaOH.
plus 0.05M EDTA. MDPA added. NMR sample in 10M NaOH in D_2O.
Chemical shift values are on the X axis. Chemical shifts of individual peaks are in green.
The Y axis indicates the intensity of response.
Bold values in black are peak areas calculated by the TopSpin software.

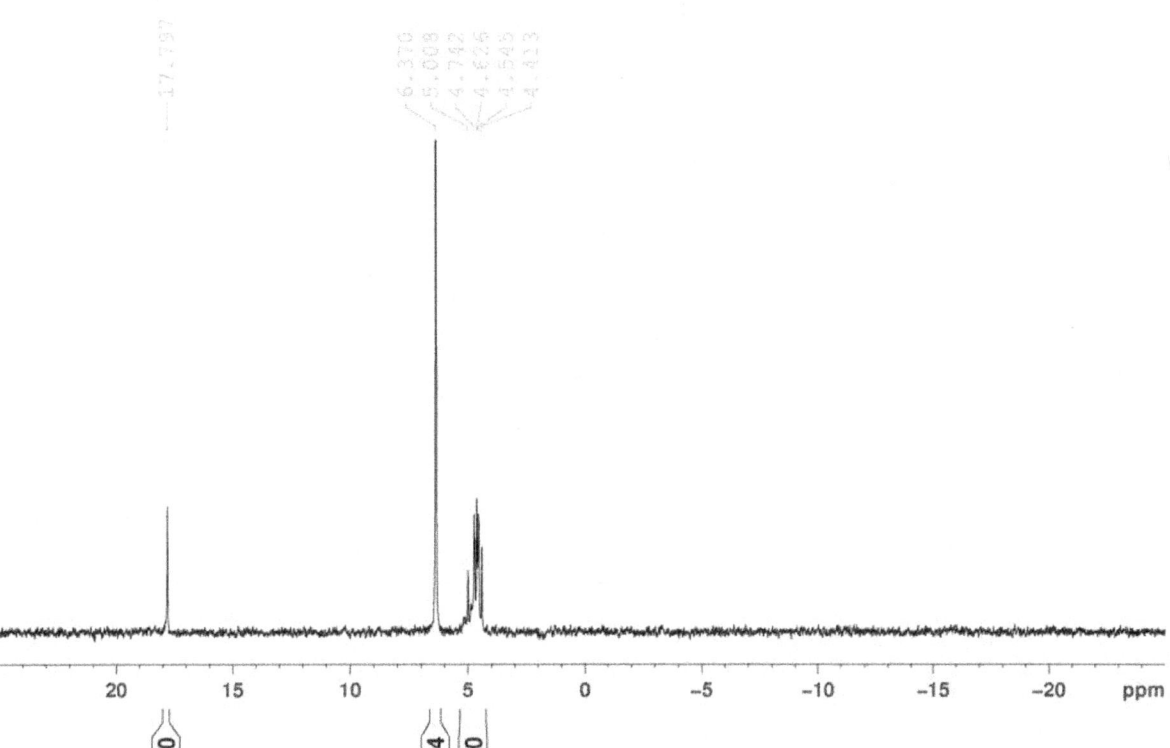

Figure 4. ^{31}P Nuclear Magnetic Resonance data for *Aphanizomenon flos-aquae* (AFA) samples collected in July and August 2010 from Upper Klamath Lake. [P, phosphorus; NMR, Nuclear Magnetic Resonance spectroscopy; AFA, cyanophyte, *Aphanizomenon flos-aquae*; M, molarity, moles per liter of solution; NaOH, sodium hydroxide; EDTA, ethylenediaminetetraacetic acid; MDPA, methylene diphosphonic acid; D_2O, deuterium oxide]—Continued

8b. ^{31}P NMR

    SB - Shoalwater Bay, AFA collected 8/9/2010, extracted with water.

    No MDPA added. NMR sample in 10M NaOH in D_2O.

    Chemical shift values are on the X axis. Chemical shifts of individual peaks are in green.

    The Y axis indicates the intensity of response.

    Bold values in black are peak areas calculated by the TopSpin software.

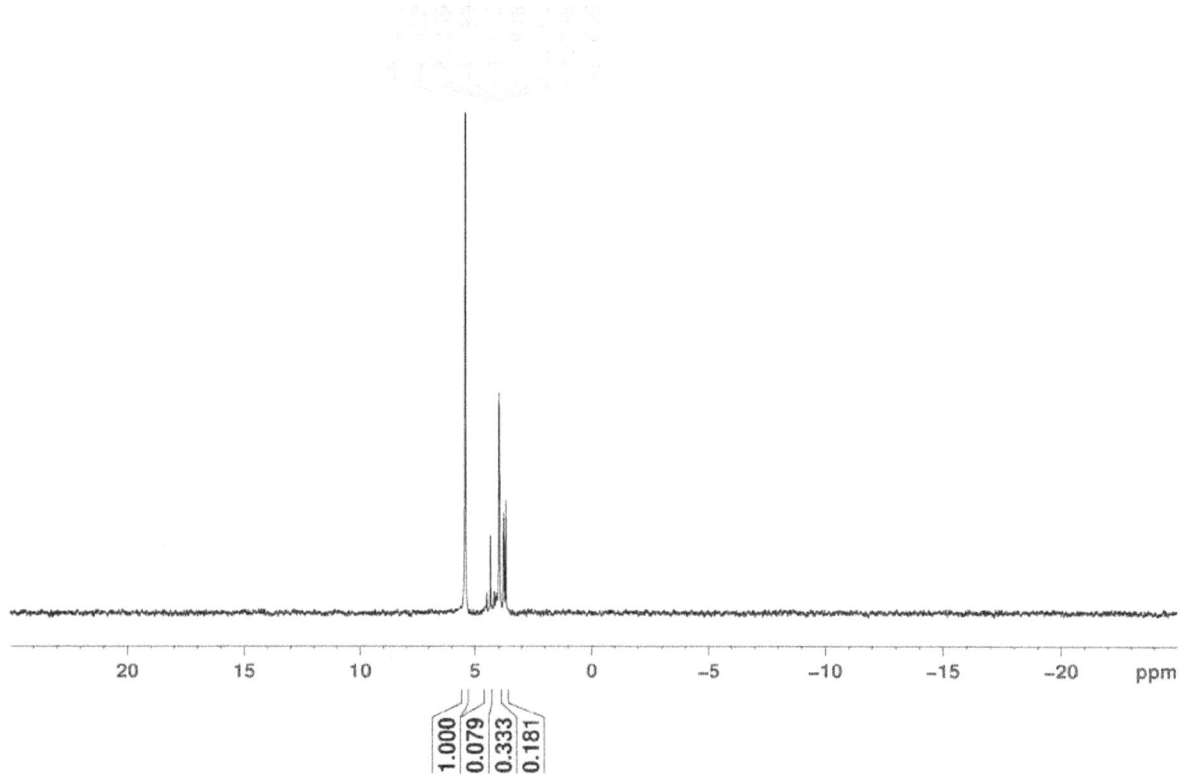

Figure 4. ^{31}P Nuclear Magnetic Resonance data for *Aphanizomenon flos-aqua*e (AFA) samples collected in July and August 2010 from Upper Klamath Lake. [P, phosphorus; NMR, Nuclear Magnetic Resonance spectroscopy; AFA, cyanophyte, *Aphanizomenon flos-aquae*; M, molarity, moles per liter of solution; NaOH, sodium hydroxide; EDTA, ethylenediaminetetraacetic acid; MDPA, methylene diphosphonic acid; D_2O, deuterium oxide]—Continued

8c. ^{31}P NMR

SB -Shoalwater Bay, AFA collected 8/9/2010, extracted with water.

MDPA added. NMR sample in 10M NaOH in D_2O.

Chemical shift values are on the X axis. Chemical shifts of individual peaks are in green.

The Y axis indicates the intensity of response.

Bold values in black are peak areas calculated by the TopSpin software.

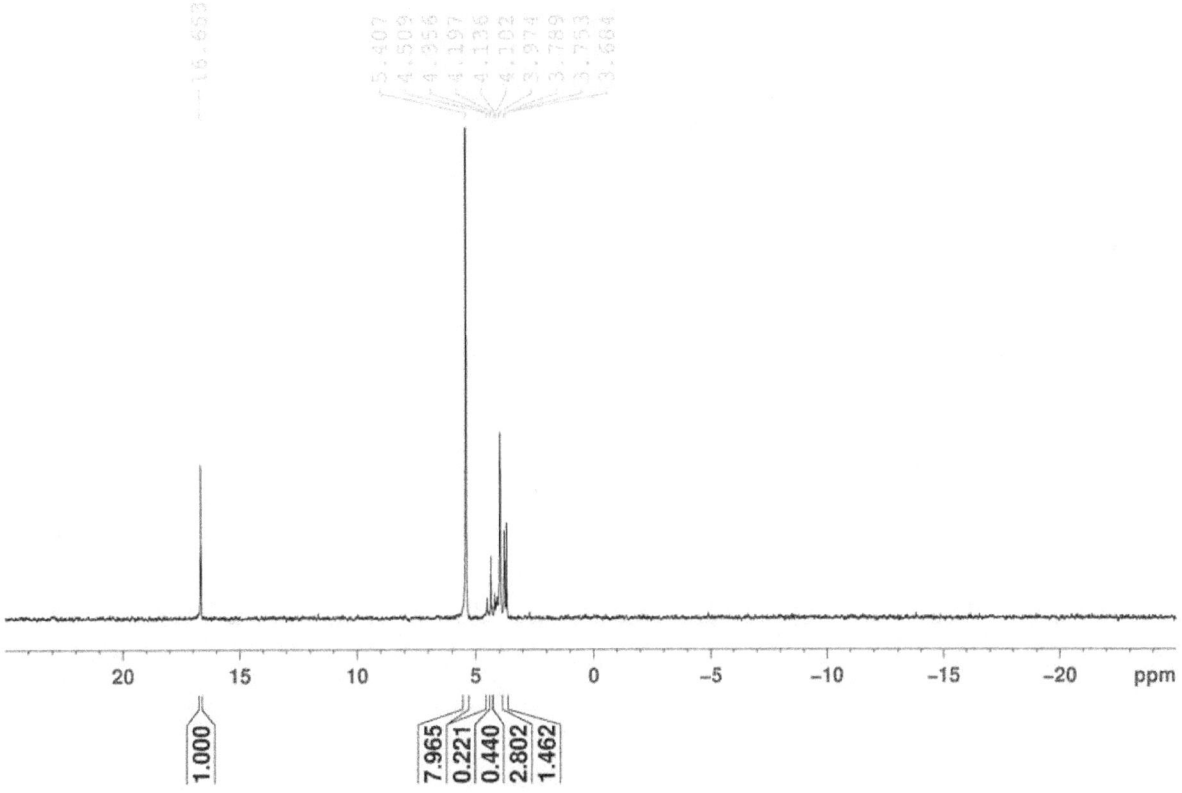

Figure 4. ^{31}P Nuclear Magnetic Resonance data for *Aphanizomenon flos-aquae* (AFA) samples collected in July and August 2010 from Upper Klamath Lake. [P, phosphorus; NMR, Nuclear Magnetic Resonance spectroscopy; AFA, cyanophyte, *Aphanizomenon flos-aquae*; M, molarity, moles per liter of solution; NaOH, sodium hydroxide; EDTA, ethylenediaminetetraacetic acid; MDPA, methylene diphosphonic acid; D_2O, deuterium oxide]—Continued

9a.   ³¹P NMR

AS - Agency Lake South Blue, AFA collected 8/9/2010, extracted with 0.25M NaOH.
plus 0.05M EDTA. MDPA added. NMR sample in 10M NaOH in D_2O.
Chemical shift values are on the X axis. Chemical shifts of individual peaks are in green.
The Y axis indicates the intensity of response.
Bold values in black are peak areas calculated by the TopSpin software.

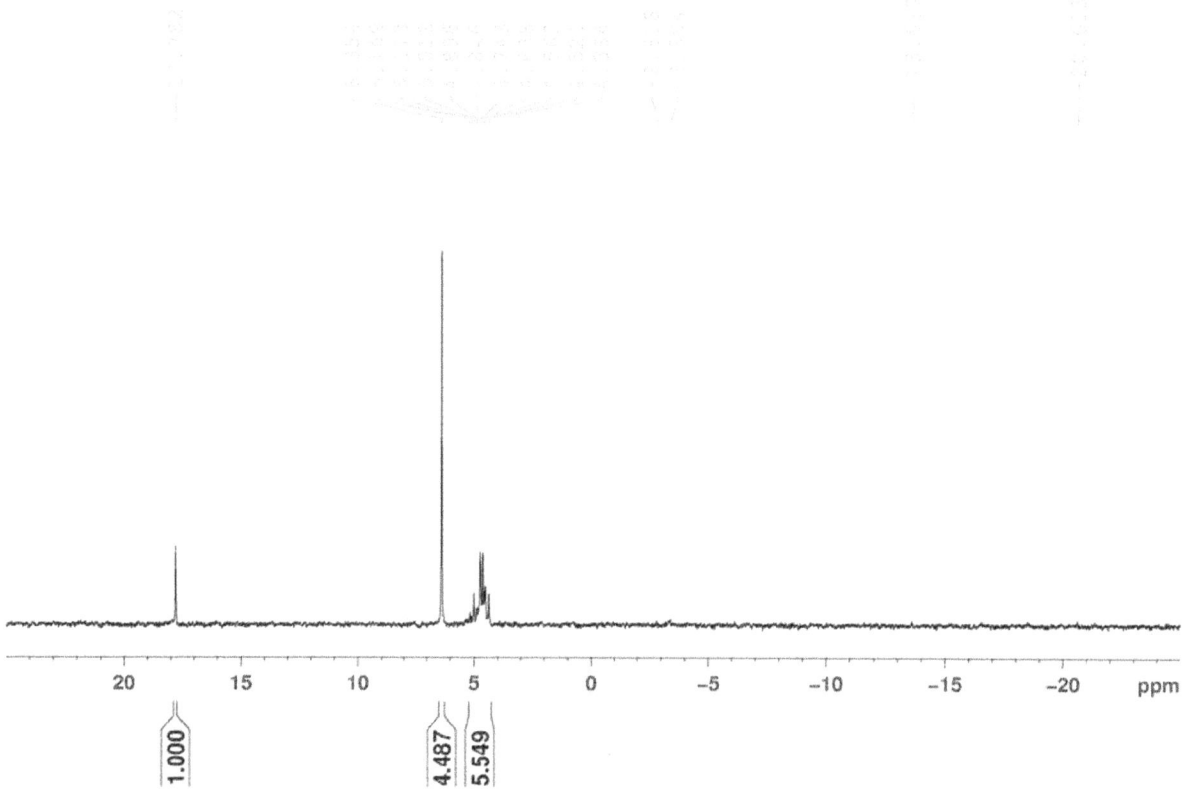

Figure 4.   ³¹P Nuclear Magnetic Resonance data for *Aphanizomenon flos-aqua*e (AFA) samples collected in July
and August 2010 from Upper Klamath Lake. [P, phosphorus; NMR, Nuclear Magnetic Resonance spectroscopy;
AFA, cyanophyte, *Aphanizomenon flos-aquae*; M, molarity, moles per liter of solution; NaOH, sodium hydroxide;
EDTA, ethylenediaminetetraacetic acid; MDPA, methylene diphosphonic acid; D₂0, deuterium oxide]—Continued

9b. ³¹P NMR

AS - Agency Lake South Blue, AFA collected 8/9/2010, extracted with water.
No MDPA added. NMR sample in 10M NaOH in D_2O.
Chemical shift values are on the X axis. Chemical shifts of individual peaks are in green.
The Y axis indicates the intensity of response.
Bold values in black are peak areas calculated by the TopSpin software

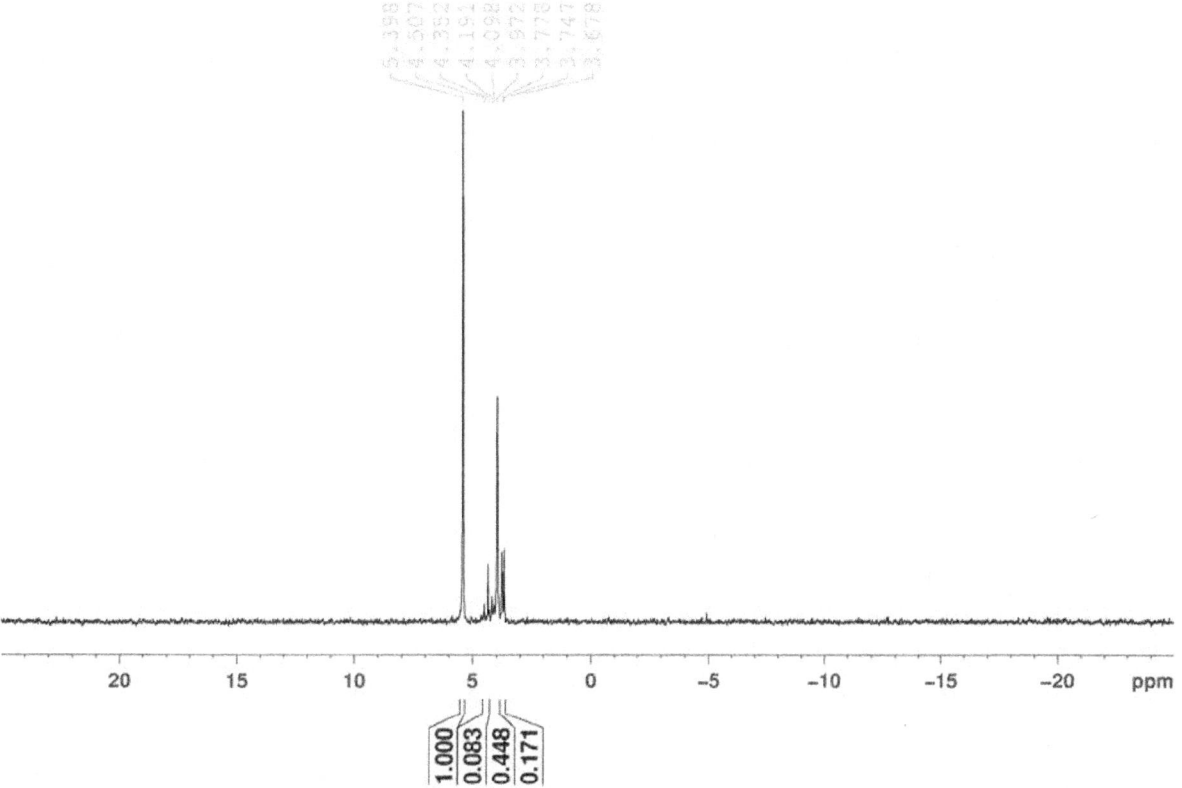

Figure 4. ³¹P Nuclear Magnetic Resonance data for *Aphanizomenon flos-aquae* (AFA) samples collected in July and August 2010 from Upper Klamath Lake. [P, phosphorus; NMR, Nuclear Magnetic Resonance spectroscopy; AFA, cyanophyte, *Aphanizomenon flos-aquae*; M, molarity, moles per liter of solution; NaOH, sodium hydroxide; EDTA, ethylenediaminetetraacetic acid; MDPA, methylene diphosphonic acid; D_2O, deuterium oxide]—Continued

9c. 31P NMR

AS - Agency Lake South Blue, AFA collected 8/9/2010, extracted with water.
MDPA added. NMR sample in 10M NaOH in D₂O.

Chemical shift values are on the X axis. Chemical shifts of individual peaks are in green.
The Y axis indicates the intensity of response.
Bold values in black are peak areas calculated by the TopSpin software.

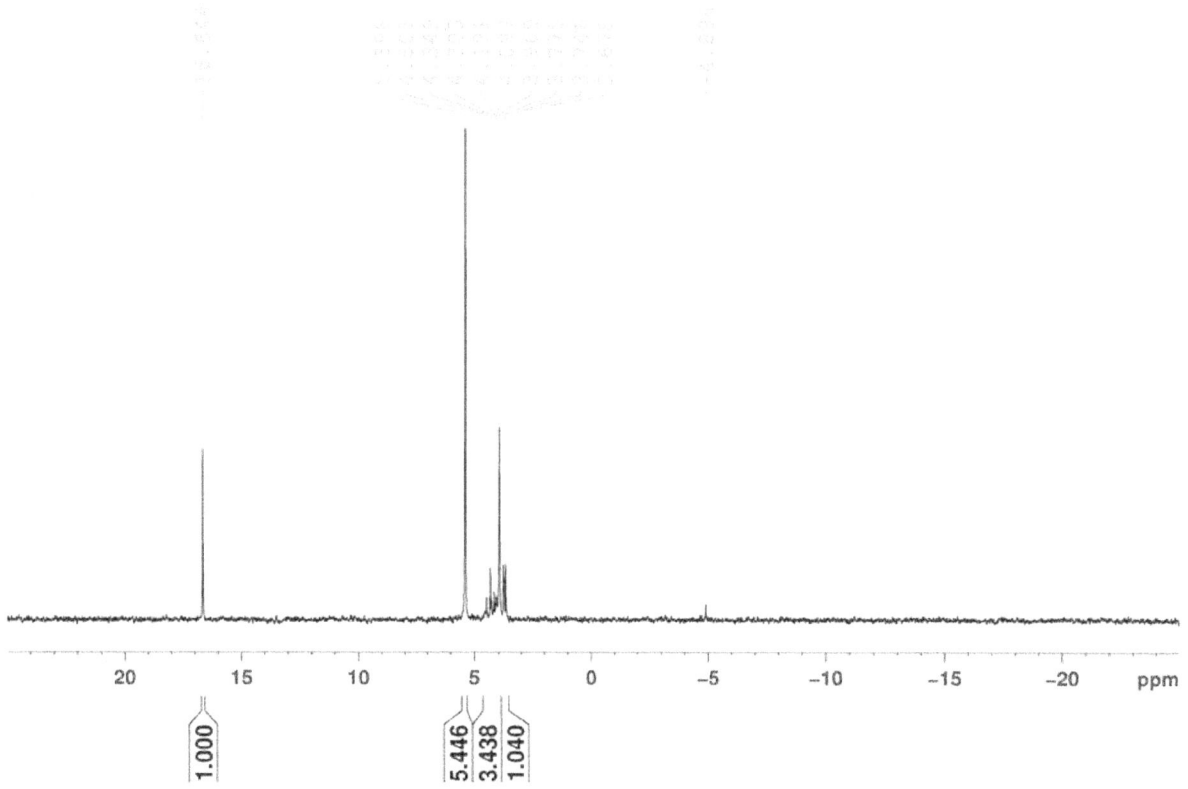

Figure 4. 31P Nuclear Magnetic Resonance data for *Aphanizomenon flos-aquae* (AFA) samples collected in July and August 2010 from Upper Klamath Lake. [P, phosphorus; NMR, Nuclear Magnetic Resonance spectroscopy; AFA, cyanophyte, *Aphanizomenon flos-aquae*; M, molarity, moles per liter of solution; NaOH, sodium hydroxide; EDTA, ethylenediaminetetraacetic acid; MDPA, methylene diphosphonic acid; D₂0, deuterium oxide]—Continued

10a. ^{31}P NMR

AS - Agency Lake South Light green, AFA collected 8/9/2010, extracted with 0.25M NaOH.
plus 0.05M EDTA. MDPA added. NMR sample in 10M NaOH in D$_2$O.

Chemical shift values are on the X axis. Chemical shifts of individual peaks are in green.
The Y axis indicates the intensity of response.

Bold values in black are peak areas calculated by the TopSpin software.

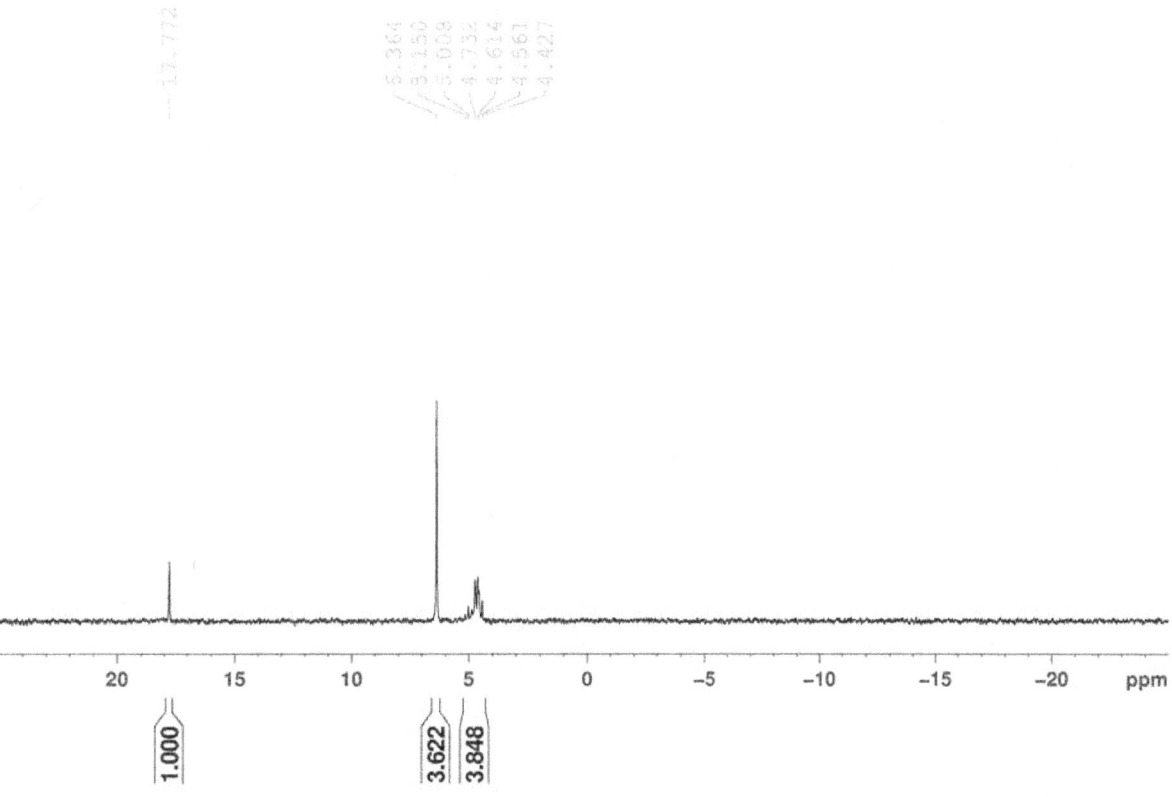

Figure 4. ^{31}P Nuclear Magnetic Resonance data for *Aphanizomenon flos-aquae* (AFA) samples collected in July and August 2010 from Upper Klamath Lake. [P, phosphorus; NMR, Nuclear Magnetic Resonance spectroscopy; AFA, cyanophyte, *Aphanizomenon flos-aquae*; M, molarity, moles per liter of solution; NaOH, sodium hydroxide; EDTA, ethylenediaminetetraacetic acid; MDPA, methylene diphosphonic acid; D$_2$O, deuterium oxide]—Continued

10b. ^{31}P NMR

AS - Agency Lake South, Light green, AFA collected 8/9/2010, extracted with water. No MDPA added. NMR sample in 10M NaOH in D$_2$O.

Chemical shift values are on the X axis. Chemical shifts of individual peaks are in green. The Y axis indicates the intensity of response.

Bold values in black are peak areas calculated by the TopSpin software.

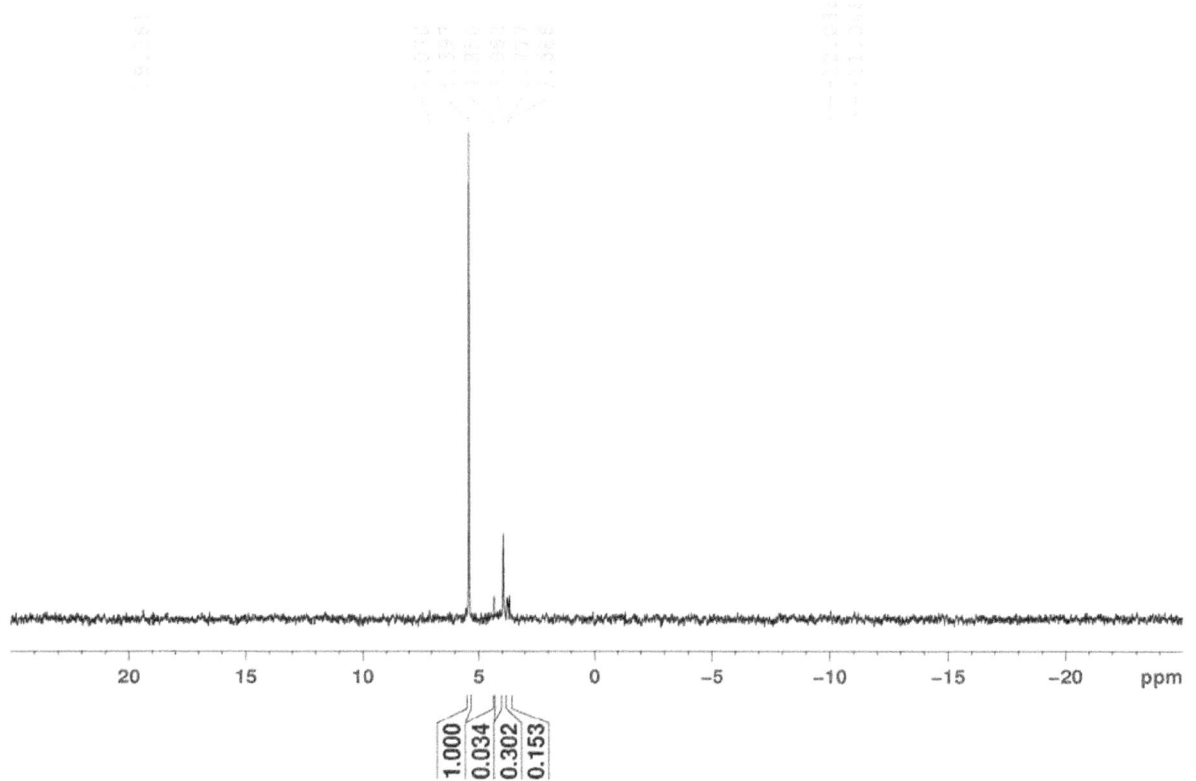

Figure 4. ^{31}P Nuclear Magnetic Resonance data for *Aphanizomenon flos-aqua*e (AFA) samples collected in July and August 2010 from Upper Klamath Lake. [P, phosphorus; NMR, Nuclear Magnetic Resonance spectroscopy; AFA, cyanophyte, *Aphanizomenon flos-aquae*; M, molarity, moles per liter of solution; NaOH, sodium hydroxide; EDTA, ethylenediaminetetraacetic acid; MDPA, methylene diphosphonic acid; D$_2$0, deuterium oxide]—Continued

^{31}P NMR

HB - Howard Bay AFA collected 8/9/2010, extracted with 0.25M NaOH.
plus 0.05M EDTA. MDPA added. NMR sample in 10M NaOH in D_2O.

Chemical shift values are on the X axis. The Y axis indicates the intensity of response.
Values in green are peak areas calculated by the TopSpin software.

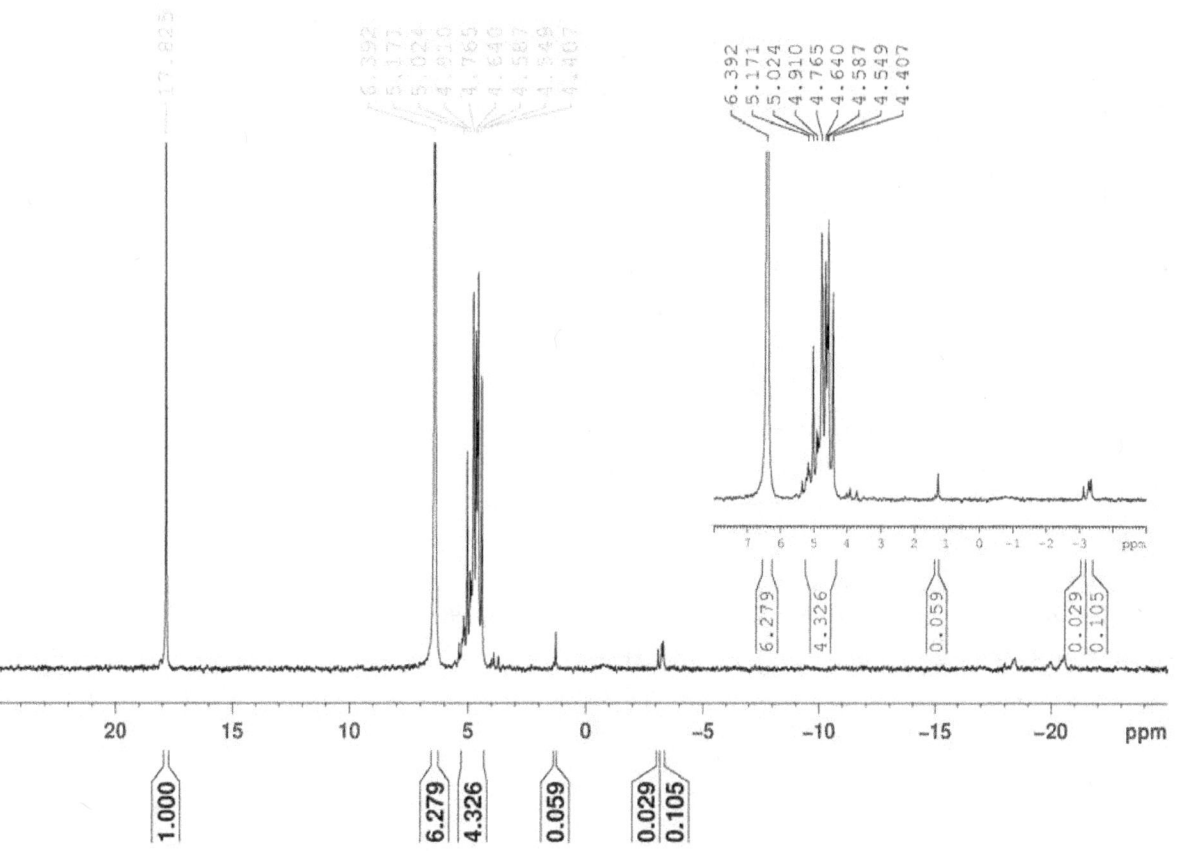

Figure 5. Spectrum 5a - ^{31}P Nuclear Magnetic Resonance spectrum of sample collected from Howard Bay (HB) in Upper Klamath Lake (UKL) on August 9, 2010. Peak at chemical shift (CS) 17.8 is the internal standard methylene diphosphonic acid (MDPA). [P, phosphorus; NMR, Nuclear Magnetic Resonance spectroscopy; AFA, cyanophyte, *Aphanizomenon flos-aquae*; M, molarity, moles per liter of solution; NaOH, sodium hydroxide; EDTA, ethylenediaminetetraacetic acid; MDPA, methylene diphosphonic acid; D_2O, deuterium oxide]

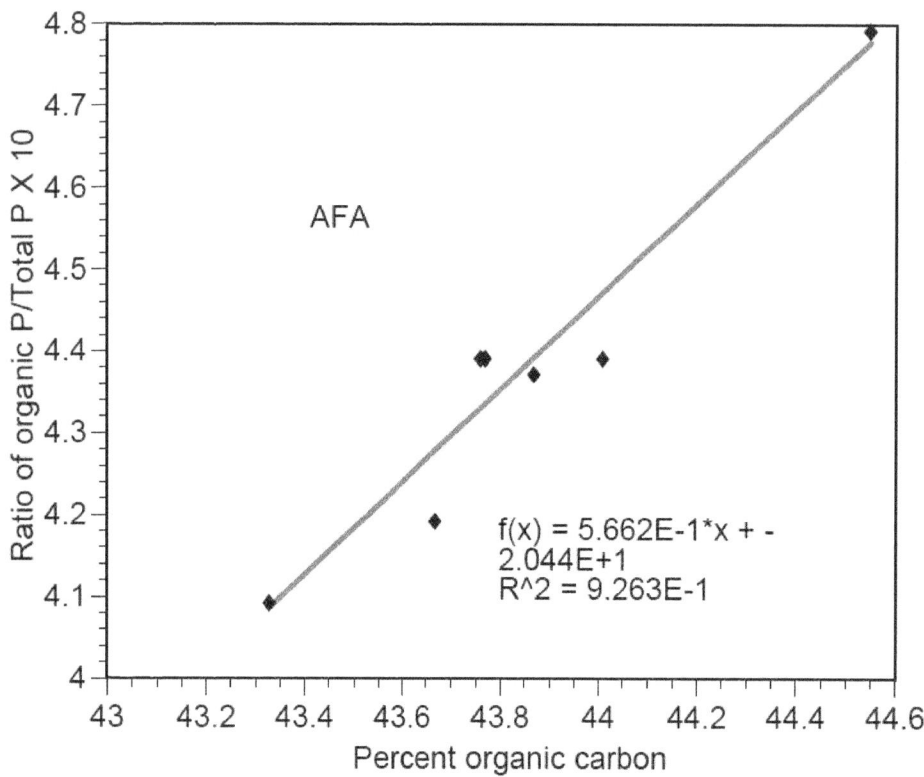

Figure 6. Ratio of concentration of organic phosphorus to the concentration of total phosphorus (TP) plotted against the percent carbon in each *Aphanizomenon flos-aquae* (AFA) sample, R^2 = 0.93. [P, phosphorus]

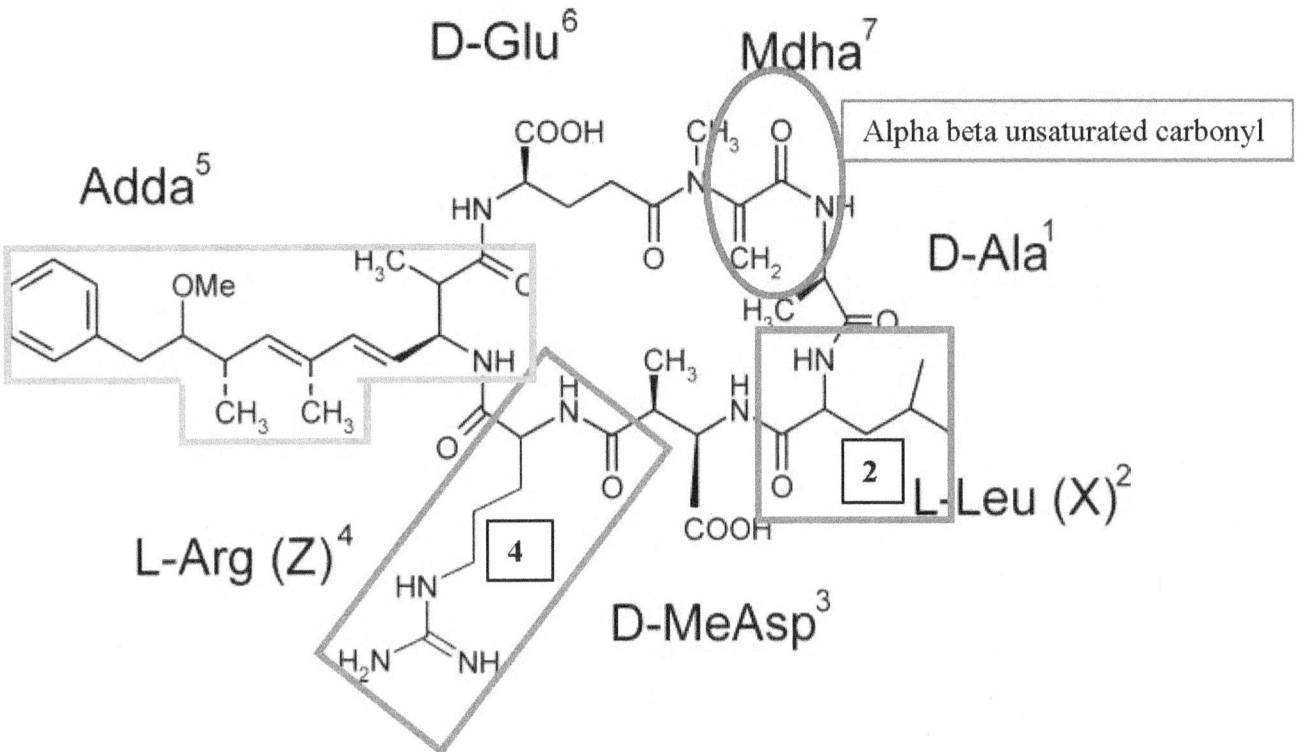

Figure 7. The seven peptide areas of the microcystin molecule include (1) D-Alanine, (2) L-Leucine, (3) D-erythro-p-methyl Asparine, (4) L-Arginine, (5) Adda, 3-amino-9-methoxy2,6,8-trimethyl-10-phenyl-4,6-decadienoic acid, (6) D-Glutamic Acid, and (7) Mdha, N-methyldehydro Alanine. Mdha contains an alpha-beta unsaturated carbonyl functional group. The X and Z amino acids vary in the homologs of microcystin but are L-leucine and L-arginine in microcystin-LR, the most common form of microcystin.

Illustration from Fewer (2007; available at *http://www.biomedcentral.com/content/pdf/1471-2148-7-183.pdf*).

Table 1. Sampling sites for *Aphanizomenon flos-aquae* collected in July and August 2012 from Upper Klamath Lake, Oregon.

Sample	Date of collection	Site	Coordinates		Decimal degrees	
1	7/27/2010	PM- Pelican Marina	N 42° 14' 16.892	W 121° 48' 37.341	N 42.24156°	W121.82341°
2	7/27/2010	PMN - Pelican Marina North	N 42° 14' 16.892	W 121° 48' 37.341	N 42.24156°	W121.82341°
3	8/9/2010	PM - Pelican Marina	N 42° 14' 16.892	W 121° 48' 37.341	N 42.24156°	W121.82341°
4	7/27/2010	NBI - North Buck Island	N 42° 18' 30.2	W 121° 51' 22.4	N 42.30823°	W121.85733°
5	8/9/2010	HB - Howard Bay	N 42° 19' 35.0	W 121° 55' 11.9	N 42.32623°	W121.92108°
6	8/9/2010	ER - Eagle Ridge	N 42° 25' 19.5	W 121° 56' 35.8	N 42.42192°	W121.94439°
7	8/12/2010	ERS - Eagle Ridge South	N 42° 25' 19.5	W 121° 56' 35.8	N 42.42192°	W121.94439°
8	8/9/2010	Shoalwater Bay	N 42° 24' 26.1	W 121° 57' 47.1	N 42.40709°	W121.96420°
9a	8/9/2010	AS - Agency Lake South (Blue color)	N 42° 31' 24.9	W121° 59' 03.4	N 42.52342°	W121.98539°
9b	8/9/2010	AS - Agency Lake South (Green color)				

Table 2. Chemical shift values for compounds that appear in ^{31}P NMR spectra.

[P, phosphorus; NMR, Nuclear Magnetic Resonance spectroscopy]

Compound	Chemical shift: Literature values	Adjustment of chemical shift using difference between chemical shift of orthophosphate observed in this experiment and the chemical shift of orthophosphate published by other authors
phosphonate methylenediphosphonic acid sodium salt	18.1***	18.1
orthophosphate monoesters	3 to 6*	4.1 to 7.1
adenosine 5 monophosphate	4.65	5.65
orthophosphate	5.7-6.1* 6.1** 7.0 to 7.1***	7.0 7.0 to 7.1
glucose-1- phosphate	3.2*	4.1
myo inositol hexakisphosphate	(5.85, 4.9, 4.6, 4.4)*	6.9, 5.9, 5.6, 5.4
orthophosphate diesters	0.25 to (-1)*	1.15 to (-.1)
DNA from salmon	(-0.5) average of two values**	0.4
RNA	0.68 and 0.56 (30 minutes after preparation) **	0.77 to 0.65
pyrophosphate	(-3.6 to -3.7)* (-4.3 to -4.4)**	(-2.5 to -2.6) (-3.4 to -3.5)
inorganic polyphosphate	(-19.2 to -20.5)***	(-19.2 to -20.5)

Koopmans and others, 2003.***
Turner and others, 2003.**
Cade-Menum, 2005.*

Table 3. ^{31}P NMR data for *Aphanizomenon flos-aquae* samples collected July–August 2010 from Upper Klamath Lake, Oregon.

[CS, chemical shift, location of peak in NMR spectrum; EDTA, ethylenediaminetetraacetic acid, metal complexing agent; Inorg, inorganic; IP, inorganic phosphorus; MDPA, methlyene diphosphonic acid, internal standard for ^{31}P NMR analysis; Inter std, internal standard; mg g-1, milligrams per gram dry weight of sample; NaOH, sodium hydroxide; NMR, Nuclear Magnetic Resonance spectroscopy; Org., organic phosphorus; OP, organic phosphorus; P, phosphorus; soln., solution; +, internal standard added; x, very small peak in spectrum]

Site and date of collection	Label on spectrum	^{31}P NMR spectrum	Extract soln.	Inter std	sample weight g	NMR CS 7 area of peak	NMR CS 7 conc of P mg g-1	NMR CS 4-6 area of peak	NMR CS 4-6 conc of P mg g-1	NMRCS 2 area of peak	NMR CS 2 conc of P mg g-1	NMR CS 0 area of peak	NMR CS 0 conc of P mg g-1	NMR CS -4 area of peak	NMR CS -4 conc of P mg g-1	NMR CS -18 area of peak	Chemical analysis TP conc of P mg g-1	% IP NMR	% OP NMR
PM - Pelican Marina	PM - Pelican Marina 7/27/10 NaOH-EDTA with MDPA	1a	NaOH-EDTA	+	0.11	5.66	2.58	5.81	2.65					0.47	0.22		5.45	0.47	0.53
7/27/2010	PM - Pelican Marina 7/27/10 Water only	1b	Water		0.112														
	PM - Pelican Marina 7/27/10 Water plus MDPA	1c	Water	+	0.114	7.40	3.26	4.14	1.82								5.09	0.64	0.36
PMN - Pelican Marina North	PMN - Pelican Marina North 7/27/10 NaOH-EDTA with MDPA	2a	NaOH-EDTA	+	0.113	6.11	2.71	4.65	2.06					0.41	0.18		4.95	0.55	0.45

Table 3. ³¹P NMR data for *Aphanizomenon flos-aquae* samples collected July–August 2010 from Upper Klamath Lake, Oregon.—Continued

[CS, chemical shift, location of peak in NMR spectrum; EDTA, ethylenediaminetetraacetic acid, metal complexing agent; Inorg., inorganic; IP, inorganic phosphorus; MDPA, methlyene diphosphonic acid, internal standard for ³¹P NMR analysis; Inter std, internal standard; mg g-1, milligrams per gram dry weight of sample; NaOH, sodium hydroxide; NMR, Nuclear Magnetic Resonance spectroscopy; OP, organic phosphorus; Org, organic; P, phosphorus; soln., solution; +, internal standard added; x, very small peak in spectrum]

Site and date of collection	Label on spectrum	³¹P NMR spectrum	Extract soln.	Inter std	sample weight g	NMR CS 7 area of peak	NMR CS 7 conc of P mg g-1	NMR CS 4-6 area of peak	NMR CS 4-6 conc of P mg g-1	NMR CS 2 area of peak	NMR CS 2 conc of P mg g-1	NMR CS 0 area of peak	NMR CS 0 conc of P mg g-1	NMR CS -4 area of peak	NMR CS -4 conc of P mg g-1	NMR CS -18 area of peak	Chemical analysis TP conc of P mg g-1	% IP NMR	% OP NMR
PMN - Pelican Marina North 7/27/10 Water only	2b		Water		0.105														
7/27/2010 PMN- Pelican Marina North 7/27/10 Water plus MDPA	2c		Water	+	0.108	6.75	3.12	3.61	1.67								4.79	0.65	0.35
PM - Pelican Bay Marina 8/9/10 NaOH- EDTA with MDPA	3a		NaOH- EDTA	+	0.098	7.56	3.88	4.48	2.30					0.67	0.34		6.51	0.59	0.41
PM - Pelican Marina 8/9/10 Water only	3b		Water		0.101														
8/9/2010 PM - Pelican Bay Marina 8/9/10 Water plus MDPA	3c		Water	+	0.109	####	4.71	2.71	1.24								5.95	0.79	0.21

53

Table 3. 31P NMR data for *Aphanizomenon flos-aquae* samples collected July–August 2010 from Upper Klamath Lake, Oregon.—Continued

[CS, chemical shift, location of peak in NMR spectrum; EDTA, ethylenediaminetetraacetic acid, metal complexing agent; Inorg., inorganic; IP, inorganic phosphorus; MDPA, methlyene diphosphonic acid, internal standard for 31P NMR analysis; Inter std, internal standard; mg g-1, milligrams per gram dry weight of sample; NaOH, sodium hydroxide; NMR, Nuclear Magnetic Resonance spectroscopy; OP, organic phosphorus; Org., organic; P, phosphorus; soln., solution; +, internal standard added; x, very small peak in spectrum]

Site and date of collection	Label on spectrum	31P NMR spec-trum	Extract soln.	Inter std	sample weight g	NMR CS 7 area of peak	NMR CS 7 conc of P mg g-1	NMR CS 4-6 area of peak	NMR CS 4-6 conc of P mg g-1	NMRCS 2 area of peak	NMR CS 2 conc of P mg g-1	NMR CS 0 area of peak	NMR CS 0 conc of P mg g-1	NMR CS -4 area of peak	NMR CS -4 conc of P mg g-1	NMR CS -18 area of peak	Chemical analysis TP conc of P mg g-1	% IP NMR	% OP NMR
NBI - North Buck Island	NBI - North Buck Island 7/27/10 NaOH-EDTA with MDPA	4a	NaOH-EDTA	+	0.103	5.93	2.87	5.30	2.56					0.25	0.12		5.55	0.52	0.48
7/27/2010	NBI - North Buck Island 7/27/10 Water only	4b	Water		0.108														
	NBI - North Buck Island 7/27/10 Water plus MDPA	4c	Water	+	0.106	6.13	2.88	3.98	1.87								4.75	0.61	0.39
HB Howard Bay	HB - Howard Bay 8/9/10 NaOH-EDTA with MDPA	5a	NaOH-EDTA	+	0.102	6.28	3.07	4.33	2.11	0.06	0.03			0.13	0.07	x	5.27	0.58	0.42
8/9/2010	HB - Howard Bay 8/9/10 Water only	5b	Water		0.103														
	HB - Howard Bay 8/9/10 Water plus MDPA	5c	Water	+	0.104	7.58	3.65	3.66	1.76	0.06	0.03			0.10	0.05	x	5.49	0.67	0.33

54

Table 3. ³¹P NMR data for *Aphanizomenon flos-aquae* samples collected July–August 2010 from Upper Klamath Lake, Oregon.—Continued

[CS, chemical shift, location of peak in NMR spectrum; EDTA, ethylenediaminetetraacetic acid, metal complexing agent; Inorg., inorganic; IP, inorganic phosphorus; MDPA, methlyene diphosphonic acid, internal standard for ³¹P NMR analysis; Inter std, internal standard; mg g-1, milligrams per gram dry weight of sample; NaOH, sodium hydroxide; NMR, Nuclear Magnetic Resonance spectroscopy; Org, organic; P, phosphorus; soln., solution; +, internal standard added; x, very small peak in spectrum]

Site and date of collection	Label on spectrum	³¹P NMR spectrum	Extract soln.	Inter std	sample weight g	NMR area of peak CS 7	NMR CS 7 conc of P mg g-1	NMR area of peak CS 4-6	NMR CS 4-6 conc of P mg g-1	NMR/CS 2 area of peak	NMR CS 2 conc of P mg g-1	NMR CS 0 area of peak	NMR CS 0 conc of P mg g-1	NMR CS -4 area of peak	NMR CS -4 conc of P mg g-1	NMR CS -18 area of peak	Chemical analysis TP conc of P mg g-1	% IP NMR	% OP NMR
ER Eagle Ridge / 8/9/2010	ER - Eagle Ridge 8/9/10 NaOH-EDTA with MDPA	6a	NaOH-EDTA	+	0.116	7.57	3.26	6.71	2.89	0.07	0.03			0.14	0.06		6.24	0.52	0.48
	ER - Eagle Ridge 8/9/10 Water only	6b	Water		0.105														
	ER - Eagle Ridge 8/9/10 Water plus MDPA	6c	Water	+	0.105	8.63	4.12	4.56	2.18	x							6.30	0.65	0.35
ERS Eagle Ridge South / 8/12/2010	ERS- Eagle Ridge South 8/12/10 NaOH-EDTA with MDPA	7a	NaOH-EDTA	+	0.107	8.53	3.98	6.28	2.93								6.91	0.58	0.42
	ERS - Eagle Ridge South 8/12/10 Water only	7b	Water		0.108														
	ERS- Eagle Ridge South 8/12/10 Water plus MDPA	7c	Water	+	0.109	####	4.62	4.51	2.08								6.70	0.69	0.31

Table 3. ^{31}P NMR data for *Aphanizomenon flos-aquae* samples collected July–August 2010 from Upper Klamath Lake, Oregon.—Continued

[CS, chemical shift, location of peak in NMR spectrum; EDTA, ethylenediaminetetraacetic acid, metal complexing agent; Inorg., inorganic; IP, inorganic phosphorus; MDPA, methlyene diphosphonic acid, internal standard for ^{31}P NMR analysis; Inter std, internal standard; mg g-1, milligrams per gram dry weight of sample; NaOH, sodium hydroxide; NMR, Nuclear Magnetic Resonance spectroscopy; OP, organic phosphorus; Org, organic; P, phosphorus; soln, solution; +, internal standard added; x, very small peak in spectrum]

Site and date of collection	Label on spectrum	^{31}P NMR spectrum	Extract soln.	Inter std	sample weight g	NMR CS 7 area of peak	NMR CS 7 conc of P mg g-1	NMR CS 4-6 area of peak	NMR CS 4-6 conc of P mg g-1	NMRCS 2 area of peak	NMR CS 2 conc of P mg g-1	NMR CS 0 area of peak	NMR CS 0 conc of P mg g-1	NMR CS -4 area of peak	NMR CS -4 conc of P mg g-1	NMR CS -18 area of peak	Chemical analysis TP conc of P mg g-1	% IP NMR	% OP NMR
SB Shoalwater Bay	SB-Shoalwater Bay 8/9/10 NaOH-EDTA with MDPA	8a	NaOH-EDTA	+	0.102	6.51	3.19	5.59	2.74								5.93	0.54	0.46
	SB - Shoalwater Bay 8/9/10 Water only	8b	Water		0.105														
8/9/2010	SB - Shoalwater Bay 8/9/10 Water plus MDPA	8c	Water	+	0.102	7.97	3.89	4.93	2.40								6.29	0.62	0.38
AS Agency Lake South	AS - Agency Lake South 8/9/10 (blue color) NaOH-EDTA with MDPA	9a	NaOH-EDTA	+	0.105	4.49	2.13	5.55	2.63								4.76	0.45	0.55
Blue	AS - Agency Lake South 8/9/10(blue color) Water only	9b	Water		0.103											x			

Table 3. ³¹P NMR data for *Aphanizomenon flos-aquae* samples collected July–August 2010 from Upper Klamath Lake, Oregon.—Continued

[CS, chemical shift, location of peak in NMR spectrum; EDTA, ethylenediaminetetraacetic acid, metal complexing agent; Inorg, inorganic; IP, inorganic phosphorus; MDPA, methlyene diphosphonic acid, internal standard for ³¹P NMR analysis; Inter std, internal standard; mg g-1, milligrams per gram dry weight of sample; NaOH, sodium hydroxide; NMR, Nuclear Magnetic Resonance spectroscopy; OP, organic phosphorus; Org, organic; P, phosphorus; soln., solution; +, internal standard added; x, very small peak in spectrum]

Site and date of collection	Label on spectrum	³¹P NMR spectrum	Extract soln.	Inter std	sample weight g	NMR CS 7 area of peak	NMR CS 7 conc of P mg g-1	NMR CS 4-6 area of peak	NMR CS 4-6 conc of P mg g-1	NMR CS 2 area of peak	NMR CS 2 conc of P mg g-1	NMR CS 0 area of peak	NMR CS 0 conc of P mg g-1	NMR CS -4 area of peak	NMR CS -4 conc of P mg g-1	NMR CS -18 area of peak	Chemical analysis TP conc of P mg g-1	% IP NMR	% OP NMR
8/9/2010	AS - Agency Lake South 8/9/10(blue color) Water plus MDPA	9c	Water	+	0.101	5.45	2.70	4.48	2.22					x			4.92	0.55	0.45
AS Agency Lake South	AS Agency Lake South 8/9/10 (green color) NaOH-EDTA with MDPA	10a	NaOH-EDTA	+	0.075	3.62	2.42	3.38	2.26								4.68	0.52	0.48
Green 8/9/2010	AS Agency Lake South 8/9/10 (green color) Water only	10b	Water		0.024														

57

Table 4. Chemical data for *Aphanizomenon flos-aquae* collected in July and August 2012 from Upper Klamath Lake, Oregon.

[TP, total phosphorus; Ca, calcium; Mg, magnesium; Ti, titanium; Al, aluminum; Fe, iron; Zn, zinc; mg g-1, milligrams per gram; wt, weight; C, carbon; N, nitrogen; C/N, ratio of carbon to nitrogen; %, percent; PM, Pelican Marina; PMN, Pelican Marina North; NBI , North Buck IslandI; HB, Howard Bay; ER, Eagle Ridge; ERS, Eagle Ridge South; SB, Shoalwater Bay; AS, Agency Lake South; na, not available; nd, not detectable]

Site and date of collection	Digest TP mg g^{-1} dry wt	Digest Ca mg g^{-1} dry wt	Digest Mg mg g^{-1} dry wt	Digest Ti mg g^{-1} dry wt	Digest Al mg g^{-1} dry wt	Digest Fe mg g^{-1} dry wt	Digest Zn mg g^{-1} dry wt	%C	%N	C/N
PM - Pelican Marina **7/27/2010**	5.24	6.15	1.96	0.01	0.05	2.98	0.05	43.9	10.0	5.1
PMN - Pelican Marina North **7/27/2010**	5.21	6.65	1.86	0.00	0.04	2.57	0.02	43.3	9.9	5.1
PM - Pelican Marina 8/9/2010	6.05	5.81	1.69	0.00	0.07	0.38	0.02	43.3	9.2	5.5
NBI - North Buck Island **7/27/2010**	5.33	6.06	2.00	0.00	0.02	0.43	nd	44.6	10.4	5
HB - Howard Bay 8/9/2010	5.42	7.12	1.61	0.00	0.07	0.50	0.02	43.7	8.5	6
ER - Eagle Ridge 8/9/2010	5.88	5.67	1.80	0.00	0.02	0.38	0.02	43.9	10.0	5.1
ERS - Eagle Ridge South 8/12/2010	6.29	6.64	1.88	0.00	0.07	0.48	0.02	44.0	9.7	5.3
SB - Shoalwater Bay 8/9/2010	5.94	5.50	1.82	0.00	0.08	0.28	0.01	43.8	9.6	5.3
AS - Agency Lake South Blue color 8/9/2010	4.66	5.83	1.66	0.00	0.00	0.38	0.02	43.8	8.0	6.4
AS - Agency Lake South Green color 8/9/2010	4.53	6.28	1.87	0.00	0.02	0.43	0.02	na		

Table 5. Degradation of microcystin in digest of *Aphanizomenon flos-aquae.*

Date of Analysis	Calculated percent degradation	
September 2, 2012	67	
September 3, 2012	45	
September 4, 2012	43	
September 29, 2012	57	
September 28, 2012	76	
	58	Average
	14	Standard deviation